EMERGENCY COMMUNICATIONS MANAGEMENT

EMERGENCY

COMMUNICATIONS

MANAGEMENT

FRANCIS X. HOLT

FIRE ENGINEERING
A PennWell Publication

Printed in the United States of America

LIBRARY OF CONGRESS CATALOGING-IN-PUBLICATION DATA

Holt, Francis X., 1949–
  Emergency communications management / by Francis X. Holt.
    p. cm.
  "A PennWell publication"—T.p. verso.
  ISBN 0-87814-918-X: $29.95
  1. Emergency communication systems—Management. 2. Fire departments—Communication systems—Management. I. Title.
TK6570.P8H65 1991
363.37'0682—dc20   90-80202
                                                                          CIP

A PENNWELL PUBLICATION

THIS BOOK is dedicated, with respect, to the late Harold Goldberg, gentleman dispatcher, and to Chief Dispatcher Russell D. Ramsey of Brooklyn Operations, who has forgotten more about how to do this job than most people ever know.

CONTENTS

LIST OF ILLUSTRATIONS

ACKNOWLEDGMENTS

OVER THE TWO YEARS of work that went into this book, many folks offered a piece of themselves.

Thanks first to my wife Debby and daughters Julie and Kate for tolerating all the times that I disappeared with my word processor, not to mention all the weekends, holidays, and nights that I was on duty. Thanks to Tom Brennan for the opportunity to work with the foremost group of fire service educators in the world. Thanks also to friends who provided feedback on ideas in the book, including Brother Myles Davis, OSF, Patricia Branley, Joe Beattie, and Steve Ahmed.

Before the book was the fire service, and there are several there whose influence contributed to the ideas I share with you. James P. McEnaney is the guy who got me started in the fire service with absolutely no idea of the trouble he was actually starting! Jerry Neville is the ultimate pragmatist/dispatcher and his attitudes are reflected frequently in my writing. Many thanks.

FRANCIS X. HOLT

ABOUT THE AUTHOR

FRANCIS X. HOLT is the owner of FXH Consulting in Wolfeboro Falls, New Hampshire. His activities include industrial training, professional growth and development seminars, and individual and group counseling. He is a registered nurse and a certified alcohol and drug abuse counselor, having studied to become both of those things while working night shifts as a dispatcher for the City of New York Fire Department.

Mr. Holt was a member of FDNY for nine-and-a-half years; for half of that time he was the president of the Fire Alarm Dispatchers Benevolent Association, the union representing FDNY dispatchers and supervisors. With the support of an active membership, as union president he was able to effect major changes in the way dispatchers worked and in the way the city viewed that work. An articulate spokesman, he made frequent appearances on local television and radio shows to advocate both the dispatchers' cause and public safety.

Mr. Holt holds bachelor's degrees in social studies and nursing and a master's degree in counseling. He is an editorial advisory board member of *Fire Engineering* magazine and lives "far from the sound of the sirens" in the Lakes Region of central New Hampshire with his wife and two daughters.

PREFACE

J UST AS NO TWO emergency communications are the same, there's no foolproof plan for success in managing your emergency communications system—only a fool would suggest that such a plan were possible. Managing the emergency communications operation is demanding and complex. Even the most experienced communications managers have difficulty making informed management decisions. Part of the problem arises from the logistics of the situation: Being "out of sight" from the rest of the department and the public you serve, it's tough to "sell" your needs when no one understands what those needs are. The other 95 percent of the difficulty lies in the scope of your operations and your ability to handle the multitude of decisions leading to your final goal: the receipt and transmission of vital information with speed and accuracy.

Ironically, many of those who rely on emergency communications—emergency responders as well as civilians—think of your operation in terms of "radios in the field." Of course, the radio sitting on the dashboard of the rig is just the tip of the iceberg; the folks charged with running emergency communications centers spend most of their time dealing with the rest of the iceberg!

This book will examine the rest of the iceberg. It will help those who are charged with managing an entire department to get a handle on the communications division that holds all the pieces together, 24 hours a day. It will help those who must make budget decisions (and those who must influence the decision makers) to bring objective intelligence to that process. It will help those responsible for planning and managing growth in the community so they're not caught short in the area of emergency response management.

Fire communications will most often be used as the basis of discussion in this book, since my practical experience was gained in the busiest fire alarm office in the world—Brooklyn, New York. However, using fire communications as a foundation does not limit this discussion to a particular emergency sector: The time pressures, the basic operating procedures, and the general management principles of fire communications, if not universal, are widely applicable to all emergency service communications operations. Furthermore, many smaller governmental districts run all of their emergency services through one combined communications center, so the means for easy transfer of the points made in this book to all emergency services is already in place.

This book will also help managers of municipalities that run their nonemergency and semiemergency services communications through their local dispatch centers. What is a "semiemergency" service? It's a service whose nonemergency responses under "normal," everyday conditions become vital to emergency organizations under extraordinary circumstances. For instance, the highway department operations are generally nonemergency; however, if a storm has blown tree limbs across the only state road in town, or if four feet of snow have dropped on you, the highway folks suddenly become absolutely essential to clear the way for ambulances, police cars, and fire engines. Points covered in this book apply to those semiemergency services as well.

Most of all, this book will help the communications manager or potential manager to create or maintain a more efficient communications center, to take a fresh approach to what is most definitely a strange business. So much of emergency communications is routine; so much is waiting for something to happen that you really don't want to happen; so much is stone-dull boring; and yet so much is frenetic-pitched excitement with life and death literally hanging in the balance. I hope that my words will guide you to make more productive use of the "boring" times and to address the needs of your dispatchers, your system, and the people and places you protect so that when crunch time comes—as we all know it will—you will be able to save lives, minimize damage to property, and go home at night feeling good about what it is you do for a living!

INTRODUCTION

BEFORE YOU READ the rest of this book, take some time to
think about the current state of your emergency communications operation in terms of its ability to deliver service to
its area of protection satisfactorily. Some key questions to consider are as follows:

Are we up-to-date technically?
This question must be asked in proper perspective. It is not
necessary, for instance, that every rural county have state-of-the-
art equipment in mobile data transmission. However, there are
operational aspects to consider. Do we have any "dead spots" in
our area of protection? Are there places where field personnel
could not reach us or hear us? Are we limiting ourselves to radios
in our technology evaluations? Will computer-assisted dispatch
help our operation within the limits of our budget? What about
our physical plant? How's our building security? How's our
emergency power supply? Is our interior lighting efficient? This
may sound silly, but do we have adequate fire exits, smoke and
heat detectors, fire extinguishers, and suppression systems? (For
many decades, the Brooklyn Central Office of FDNY had only
one door, and it was at the front of the building where the
furnace, kitchen, computer room, and garbage storage were—
near the likely sources of ignition and fire loading. The dispatchers, however, worked at the far end of the building, where
there was no fire exit. Needless to say, this condition was corrected, or I'd be too embarrassed to write about it!)
There are also administrative aspects to consider when evaluating your technical proficiency. Generally, these can be cov-

ered by asking yourself if you are getting the most for your money. For instance, are our bid specifications meeting our needs? Are we sticking with one local vendor because we've done business with him for 20 years while the folks in the next county are advertising bids in papers 300 miles away and getting more bang for their buck?

Do we have a quality-assurance mechanism?

Ask yourself: Are we content in our methods because that's the way it's always been done or do we constantly examine the critical aspects of our operation? Do we measure response times and catalog citizen complaints? Do we run postoperation communications critiques after our major incidents? Do we periodically review and update our operations manual? Is our list of available equipment and their locations kept current? Is our notifications list kept current? Are our "key personnel" rosters checked quarterly for accuracy of phone numbers? Do we subject each form we use to a yearly reappraisal for completeness and efficiency? Most important, do we encourage our "line troops" to identify weak links in our operation? I know that this is communications we're talking about, but *do we listen?*

Are we successful in keeping our employees productive?

The link between the public and the field forces is the dispatcher. If he does not function optimally, the most sophisticated equipment in the world is not going to compensate. Ask yourself: How does our sick leave and injury experience measure up? Do we have a grievance procedure? How often is it used? Are our job descriptions accurate and comprehensive? Does each member know what he is supposed to do, what is expected of him? Do we have a formal training program or do we rely primarily on on-the-job training? Do we recognize excellence in performance? Are our salaries competitive? Do we have a clear-cut career promotional ladder or do our dispatchers find themselves in a career dead-end? What is our turnover rate? Do our schedules meet service demands *and* personnel demands?

Does everyone else know what we're doing here?

By "everyone else" I mean the field personnel who are on the other end of the communications; the mayor and city council who may be reluctant to fund a new dispatcher's position but who won't hesitate to scream when the phone rings four times when they call; and the citizens whose taxes pay the freight.

Are we aware of and can we handle growth in our area of protection?

Look around your area and see if there are new subdivisions, new factories, new occupancies in old buildings. Ask yourself: Do we keep up with building permits and with street names? Is our record keeping haphazard or do we assign a member to stay on top of it? Is somebody going to call in a fire some day only to have our dispatcher say, "Where is that?" Are we going to have a whole subdivision ready for occupancy and find that the nearest fire alarm box is a mile away?

Now that you have asked yourself these questions and have heightened your awareness of what in your emergency communications operation may need overhauling or simply tuning up, let's take a look at some of the answers. As we do, keep in mind the national and state laws, standards, and recommended standards that you'd be wise to consider from the standpoints of management efficiency and legal liability. For example, the National Fire Protection Association's *NFPA 1221: Standard for the Installation, Maintenance and Use of Public Fire Service Communication Systems* covers many aspects of communications centers, particularly in the more technical areas of operations. The Fair Labor Standards Act is an act of Congress that imposes some very well-defined rules regarding the employer–employee relationship, and definitely concerns you as a manager or prospective manager. Your familiarity with these and other laws and standards could be vital to your career and your sanity.

CHAPTER ONE

The Center Itself

ALTHOUGH THE PROSPECT of building a new communications center is attractive, most managers won't have the funds or the need to do so. However, many centers around the country are renovated each year for many reasons, some of which are to accommodate growth, to combine or separate police and fire operations (depending on the situation there are good reasons to do either), and, most commonly, to accommodate new equipment. There are also hundreds of centers that don't require costly renovations but nevertheless could be improved substantially if you take the time to view your operation from a fresh perspective. You may need the help of a new pair of eyes—a consultant's perhaps—to do that effectively. The fact that the communications center is such a fixture in the department and in the community quite naturally can cloud the manager's objectivity. But whether or not someone does the "seeing" for you, take a few steps out of the forest so that you can see the trees you've been living with for years.

PHYSICAL PLANT

LOCATION

The emergency communications center most often is located in the physical plant of general governmental operations. It may occupy a section of a county complex or a separate floor or part of a floor in police or fire headquarters. Sometimes it's simply a room in the back of town hall. Whatever the case may be, the location of your emergency communications center is one of those things that you tend to just accept as always being there—if that's where it is, then that's where it is, right?

Well, not exactly. Your location is a significant factor in your ability to provide service. Examine your location as it pertains to every facet of your organization. If your location isn't compatible with the service demands of your community, then change may be in order. Determine whether your location really suits your needs. Does it give rise to recurring problems in such areas as security and personal safety that inhibit the effectiveness of your staff? There may be alternative locations—perhaps already owned by the municipality—that better suit your needs. Locational problems sometimes can be overcome by modifying the internal layout or the structure itself, but if moving the operation is necessary, have you consulted with engineers to determine whether the new location allows for quality radio communications? Changing the location of your communications center requires consideration of dozens of factors (for instance, as stated in NFPA 1221, "The floor elevation shall be above the 100-year flood plain prediction") that you wouldn't have to think about at any other time in your career, but God help you if you don't: They could come back to haunt you. Location is fundamental to your operation, and it can be the most troublesome. Give it a good, hard look.

SECURITY

Regardless of whether or not your operation is housed in the ideal structure dedicated solely to the purpose of communications, security is a primary concern that's shaped by the particular characteristics of your location and your operational needs.

Security is far more involved than simply choosing locks for the doors. Consider, for example, the sign on the building. When it comes to identifying emergency communications centers for what they actually are, there are two schools of thought. One says that clearly identifying the building (as the public safety building or whatever) does a service to the taxpayers who can see their tax dollars at work and have a place to go if they need any sort of assistance, 24 hours a day. On the other hand, some communications center personnel are horrified by the thought of putting the name on the building or identifying its function in any way. Those in the security business identify the emergency communications center as a very sensitive location, a nerve center that, among other things, could be considered a potential target for terrorists. In preparation for Liberty Weekend in New York City in 1986, the FDNY Starfire computer-assisted dispatch center in lower Manhattan, which ties together and displays the current working operations of the five borough central offices, was placed on severely restricted access for weeks before the Fourth of July celebration. To a lesser degree, there are those in busy communications centers who simply wouldn't have the time for the traffic that would result from building identification. "People who are walking by here think this is a Parks Department building," said a supervising dispatcher at FDNY's Brooklyn Central Office. "It's just as well, because we don't have time here to be answering the doorbell for every guy who comes along and wants directions or a permit."

Of course, it is often hard to disguise a building's purpose when it has a 250-foot antenna behind it and red cars in the parking lot. Sometimes, however, even those clues can be misinterpreted. A few years back, on a slow night tour in the Brooklyn Central Office, I and another dispatcher answered the doorbell at 4:30 in the morning. (It was not considered wise for only one man to answer the door in that neighborhood at that time!) A gentleman stood before us, grinning and clutching a brown paper shopping bag. We asked if we could help him. "I saw the antenna out back. I know what you guys are doing here," he said. We knew that, in addition to the "buffs" who really appreciated the work we did, there were some misguided souls who listened to the radio all night—a lot of them called us when they had nothing to do. We figured that this guy might be one of them.

So, okay, he guessed that this nondescript building on the edge of the Brooklyn Botanical Gardens was the FDNY Brooklyn Central Office. So why was he here at 4:30 in the morning? When he reached into his shopping bag, we jumped to restrain him; we both had seen too many weapons come out of surprising places. However, this gent was not pulling out a knife or a gun—he was pulling out hundreds of pictures of flying saucers. "I know that you're talking to them. I found out. I heard you on my receiver." In the end, we could only get rid of the guy by allowing him to continue to "listen in on our conversations with aliens" and to promise to "keep our secret." The moral of the story is that the security of your building—and, thus, the entire operation dependent on what's housed in that building—can be breached in many pointless, unexpected, and unusual ways.

You try to prepare for as many threats as possible. After all, Murphy's Law is why you have a job! But for each security measure you take there is usually some trade-off that affects other, sometimes not immediately apparent aspects of your operation. Take the matter of windows in the emergency communications center. For centers that are below ground, such as the Philadelphia Fire Department's Spring Garden Street headquarters, windows are obviously not an issue. But for aboveground operations, particularly at street level, windows can be a thorny problem. FDNY's Manhattan Central Office is located in Central Park. Across the street from the office is a large outcropping of rock, some 25 feet high. From the top of that ledge, some local little darlings could easily pitch rocks through the Central Office windows. And they did. So Manhattan had its windows gated and boarded. Aside from the obvious fire hazard involved, there was also a significant alteration of the work environment. Dispatchers detailed from other boroughs to work in Manhattan reported a sense of working in a "bunker." They felt closed in. Some felt they had no sense of the passage of time and that the experience was disorienting.

Other aspects of a "no-windows" policy that indirectly affect dispatch operations are not as obvious at first. In fact, awareness of the "outside world" affects a lot of dispatcher decision making. Factors such as snow, rain, darkness, and wind all influence how a dispatcher will evaluate certain kinds of calls for assistance. A dispatcher who is physically detached from those stimuli, aside from perhaps being somewhat compromised in his sense of mental well-being, is not as currently well-informed about his area of protection as he might be.

How can this make a difference? Take the situation in Staten Island, where half a million people living on 755 miles of streets in a 57-square-mile area are protected by 28 fire companies, meaning that, once you get beyond the first-due engine and truck on the alarm assignment, you sometimes are talking about a longer response time than is expected in other parts of New York City. A lot of Staten Island is particularly hilly terrain, and while it offers some dreamy views of New York Harbor, response time in certain weather conditions can be nightmarish. A dispatcher who receives a call for an occupied structure fire and has a "feeling" about the call—if he is aware of an ice storm that has struck in the past 20 minutes and knows his area of protection well enough to know that the address given is at the crest of a steep incline—may start out companies from both sides of the hill, even if the normal assignment only calls for the closer companies on the steeper side of the hill. The dispatcher who's aware of the weather knows that the companies coming from a farther distance but up a gentler incline may have the best chance of getting there first.

In rural areas, the same type of dispatcher-altered response can be seen in the spring "mud season." When thawing snow and ice conditions are worsened by a sudden downpour, many unpaved roads are turned into impassable rivers of mud. It is sometimes the case that companies coming from farther away but on paved roads will stand a better chance of getting to the scene at all. But in order for a dispatcher to alter a response for these reasons, he must be in touch with the environment in the first place.

Another consideration when dealing with windows is whether or not you plan to install a computer-assisted dispatch system. The relative position of the windows and the CRT (cathode ray tube) screens can cause a glare that makes it impossible for the dispatcher to work. More about that in Chapter Seven.

Of course, there are "window" stories from both sides of the issue. Dispatchers have been shot at simply because they provided a tempting silhouette for some maniac on the street. And I was in the Bucks County, Pennsylvania Emergency Dispatch Center—located high atop the county office building, which in turn is situated on a high elevation—when a dispatcher was able to act like a forest firetower watchman and spot "a smoke" on the horizon. So obviously there are good and bad points to windows, just as there are positives and negatives about identifying your building.

Other security considerations include closed-circuit television cameras, remote-controlled electronic locks, and identification badges for personnel and visitors. In all cases, the need for specific security measures is determined by the nature of your operation and its setting. The trick, though, is establishing who defines those criteria and how. You cannot act on the "we've always done it this way and there hasn't been a problem yet" philosophy. How many times have you heard a probie in the firehouse say something like, Gee, it's quiet tonight? And how long does it take the veterans to jump on him for tempting fate? So why tempt fate with your communications operation? Unless you're the type to point out to the pitcher that he has a no-hitter going, you are going to look at your own "no-hitter" ("There hasn't been a problem yet") as a bit of good fortune and not as a reason for neglecting to take a good, hard look at your security system.

You may not need closed-circuit TV, but at least consider how it might make your operation better. Sensors in your driveway or parking lot *might* be ridiculous, but just give it a look so that you can sharpen your perspective. You may have commissioned local contractors to handle past work on your building, but do you know all their subcontractors? Especially if you follow some of the quality-assurance advice later in this book and seek bids from many vendors, you'll realize that there is an increased likelihood that some of the people working on your renovation or installation work are not local folks who are known to everybody. It does not take a lot of effort to stipulate in a contract that all workers will pick up identification badges from the shift supervisor at the beginning of their day and will turn them in as they go home. It will, however, increase your facility's security, not only by controlling who is coming and going in a sensitive area but also by giving a clear message that you are serious about security. This in itself has a high deterrent value to potential "bad guys." It also enhances employee morale: They see concrete evidence that what they do is valuable to the community. (Appreciation for their work is always evident in a disaster, but it's not always shown for the less intense events that compromise the majority of the work they do.) In some locations, your employees will feel better knowing that it is more difficult for people to rip off their cars or to attack them after work.

A final consideration in the overall security of your building is that of the exposures—the immediately adjacent occupancies. If yours is an attached building, you will, because of both the essential nature of your work and the amount of money invested in the plant, have a keen interest in the fire safety measures undertaken by your neighbors!

SAFETY

It is a little like the doctor taking the cigar out of his mouth to tell you to stop smoking: Quite often we find that the people in the public safety business don't look after their own safety! There are many reasons for this. A subconscious sort of smugness is one. After all, this *is* the fire department—what could go wrong here? Also, in many cases the building that houses the communications center was neither designed nor modified to keep up with the evolution of the emergency communications business. Consideration may not have been given to such vital fire protection and operational items as fire exits; adequate wiring and automatic fire suppression systems for CAD (although halon systems are the most widely used, the communications manager would do well to consider the Environmental Protection Agency's position regarding that extinguishing agent: Regulations are in effect so that by 1992 all production of halon will be frozen at 1986 levels, and further legislation to phase out halon completely between the years 2000 and 2005 has been proposed); and sufficient emergency lighting, cooling, and heating systems.

FIRE SAFETY

It is usually a good idea to ask your district's fire department to inspect the physical plant as if it were any high-risk commercial occupancy to which they might some day have to respond. I say "usually" because there are always political considerations that need to be clarified. You don't need the local company officer using his inspection report to bash the communications officer. You don't need the union using the inspection as grist for a press release just prior to negotiations. What you do need is an honest appraisal of the plant. It must be made clear by the department's upper management that this is what they want. Frequently, a department's leaders will view a negative inspection report of one of their own facilities as an indication of failure, suggestive of poor management, or worse, a personal attack. The *really* poor manager is the one who would discourage or hide such a report. A good manager wants his people to know that he is concerned for their safety. He wants the taxpayers to know that he is protecting their investment in the building and equipment that represents their first line of defense in all kinds of emergencies. He will act to correct whatever deficiencies are uncovered in an honest assessment of his building.

If you have not been inspecting your facility periodically and if, as is the case in so many communications centers, you find that much of your physical plant has been retrofitted to accommodate technical developments in the field, you may want a professional safety engineer to perform the initial inspection. Then after his report, department personnel should continue the process of maintaining the same level of fire safety that you expect from the public you protect.

MEDICAL SAFETY

It is a good idea to train dispatching personnel in cardiopulmonary resuscitation techniques and in the use of a trauma kit and resuscitator. These skills are useful for many reasons, not the least of which is the amount of stress associated with the job. Such preparation will also prove to be an asset if you publicly identify the purpose of your building and persons present themselves at the door with medical emergencies.

INJURY PREVENTION

While I was president of the union that represented FDNY fire alarm dispatchers and their supervisors, I handled a large number of grievances that arose from dangerous working conditions. These ranged from improperly installed electrical equipment to malfunctioning kitchen appliances to holes in the floor, broken windows, and defective chairs. I have no doubt that, if asked a theoretical question regarding safety in the workplace, the department's upper-level managers would have responded appropriately. However, in practice their areas of responsibility were often dangerous to the people working there. Why the disparity between what they wanted and what they had? The primary reason was that an atmosphere of safety consciousness had not been established. Upper-level managers (communications chief, commissioners) were insulated from the day-to-day operations of their communications offices by several layers of middle managers (borough chief dispatchers, chief of operations) who were not inculcated with any *active* concern for safety of the workplace. This resulted in lost man-hours because of injury, increased overtime costs to replace injured personnel, and a substantial amount of labor-relations dollars spent in processing the grievances. And all of this money was aside from whatever it cost to correct the original condition.

There are no other fire communications operations on the scale of FDNY, but each political organization has its own layers of insulation. It would be pathological for anyone to wish that unsafe conditions existed; however, dangers can grow when no emphasis is placed on their eradication. Just as you have periodic fire inspections, so should you have monthly safety inspections. After a few months you should be able to develop a checklist for this purpose (see Figure 1-1). Any checklist not only should include the obvious categories such as fire extinguishers, smoke detectors, circuit breakers, HVAC system, furnishings, and building integrity (windows, fences, security systems), it also

Figure 1-1
MONTHLY SAFETY/MAINTENANCE CHECKLIST

	Satisfactory	Unsatisfactory
Fire extinguisher pressure		
Smoke detectors		
Circuit breakers		
Heating, Ventilation, and Air Conditioning		
Ground Fault Interrupters		
Building Integrity:		
windows		
fences		
security systems		
Furnishings:		
tables		
chairs		
appliances		

Review of last month's unsatisfactory conditions: Corrected?

Description of Condition	Yes	No
1.		
2.		
3.		
4.		

Any safety grievances initiated or workers' compensation claims filed since time of last inspection?

must provide some means of referring back to previous inspections. Thus it is productive to list all unsafe conditions noted on earlier inspections, along with a note regarding their disposition. If a noted condition is not resolved, an explanation should be attached. Furthermore, your safety checklist should make reference to any safety-related grievances, on-the-job injuries, and workers' compensation claims filed since the time of the last inspection. If you have more than one communications center in your jurisdiction, it will prove useful to include references to injuries, grievances, and claims in other facilities with an eye toward preventing them in your own. A similar preventive stance can be taken by an association of communications officers that shares experiences productively. As anybody in the fire service knows, prevention is a whole lot easier than intervention.

NOISE

Communications personnel depend on a lot of audio stimuli. It is an intrinsic part of the job. They pick up the phones when they ring. They react to buzzers when alarm boxes are pulled. They respond to the calls of field units on the radio. They monitor the frequencies of adjacent jurisdictions and other agencies on scanners.

The dispatcher's listening is not the same as that of other people. If he picks up a ringing phone and still hears other lines ringing, it sets the tone for the speed of his conversation. Since a dispatcher cannot assess the degree of urgency until he either has made contact with a caller or hears many alarm boxes ringing in from the same area, his ears are always attuned to what is happening around him in the communications center. It helps him set priorities (for example, to a person complaining about an open fire hydrant he might say, "I'm going to put you on hold; I have a fire phone ringing."). He can, while operating the radio, synthesize dozens of clues around him into the most efficient channel of communications. He knows which of the fire tickets sitting in front of him (or flashing on a CRT) has gotten the most calls and which presents the greatest life hazard. After years of dealing with fire officers he will be able to tell by tone and delivery which call is the most urgent. The dispatcher knows that this is not as easy as it sounds, since the folks in the field are all experienced professionals and there are no hysterics involved, even when they are faced with overwhelming chaos. A casual listener will not be able to tell if the calling unit has arrived at a nonstructural fire or an occupied, multiple-dwelling structure with people hanging out of all the windows. But the dispatcher has developed the "ear" that makes the entire operation easier.

If he is to keep that "ear," it must be treated with respect! So many communications centers are such a cacophony of buzzers, bells, chimes, and radio speakers, it is a wonder that the dispatchers all don't go home with headaches every night. The trick is to balance the degree of audio stimulation so that you will reduce occupational stress while maintaining a sufficient level of awareness among staff members. If yours is a large and busy communications center, then you may wish to tone down some of the signaling devices. Before FDNY renovated all five of its central offices to accommodate CAD, I can remember sitting somewhat helplessly at the radio console watching another dispatcher *shouting* additional data for an alarm that I had in front of me. The problem was that there were several major fires erupting concurrently, and so was the Brooklyn Central Office; I simply could not hear the dispatcher on the other side of the room! He had to remove himself from the console at which he was receiving alarms and run around the room to the radio console in order for me to get the critical information on the air.

Besides the obvious operational impediment and physiological stress created by noise, the main thing you wish to avoid is a psychological attentuation or "tuning out" to the *sound* of alarms (the question of attentuation to the *content* of those calls is addressed in the stress management section of Chapter Six).

However, if yours is a relatively small operation you may want to put your all—electronically and otherwise—into each alarm that comes in, making sure that nobody misses anything. In some operations, any conversation that takes place on a fire phone (that is, one which is dedicated to emergency calls as separate from administrative communication) is automatically fed through wall speakers so that other personnel will hear the details and start the dispatch process even before the caller gets off the phone. In jurisdictions where thousands of calls are received, this method becomes counterproductive rather rapidly.

CRISIS OPERATIONS

To a large degree, the ease with which your emergency communications unit functions in a crisis hinges on how well your planners are aware of the relationship between crisis functioning and your physical plant. Pick your crisis: civil unrest, natural disaster, labor dispute, nuclear accident. No matter what it is, you'll do better if your physical plant has been considered when planning a response to it.

CIVIL UNREST

Although the possibility is always there, civil unrest does not have to follow the classic "race riot" model of the sixties. Today it could mean an unruly mob after a rock concert, picketers blocking the entrance to a nuclear plant, or a "celebration" of a sports championship. In larger cities or places where events of international significance are taking place (summits, conferences, chess matches, sporting events), it might mean dealing with the consequences of a systematic terrorist attack.

With regard to civil disturbances, emergency communications center plant considerations generally fall into three categories: integrity of the building, sustenance of the personnel in it, and two-way access to commercial radio and television stations.

Integrity of the building includes all of the security precautions noted earlier in this chapter as well as the NFPA-required second source of power to keep your operation humming.

Sustenance of your personnel includes adequate food and water for prolonged operations. It also includes adequate backup for heating and cooling systems, since temperature extremes contribute to fatigue and tired people make mistakes. A rest area, away from the operations area but with intercom capacity to recall dispatchers to the work area if needed, is also indicated for prolonged operations. And no matter what your normal operating expectations are for night tours (most jurisdictions take disciplinary action against communications personnel sleeping on duty), cots for catnaps are necessary.

Two-way access to commercial radio and television stations is needed for several reasons. Minicam technology allows on-the-scene TV crews to beam live images that can help emergency communications personnel get a current picture of what is happening. It helps if your communications personnel are as aware of current events as are the viewers at home who may wind up calling your operations center, looking for direction in time of disaster. Such awareness can sometimes trigger an official pre-emptive statement that can decrease your workload. The fire commissioner or the mayor may go on the air to tell people not to call in trash fires or auto fires since the department is not responding to them, or to ask people not to call in the burning vacant warehouse by the river since it is in an unsecure area and—given that no life hazard is involved—it is safer to let it burn. A surprising number of people actually call emergency communications centers when they either hear sirens or see a distant column of smoke to ask what's going on! Official communication from the department can prevent such telephone tie-ups.

NATURAL DISASTER

Identify your geographical likelihood, be it tornadoes, earthquakes, hurricanes, floods, avalanches, or forest fires. Then take a closer look at whether or not some *unlikely* service demands could occur in your area. If you check the records in your area, you may be surprised to find that you are vulnerable to natural disasters. Folks in New Hampshire often are surprised when a powerful twister comes roaring off one of their lakes and moves a garage or two. Similarly, rural firefighters often are surprised to hear that FDNY—considered a strictly urban fire department— faces some of its heaviest service demands during the twice-yearly brushfire seasons on Staten Island.

Staten Island is a part of New York City that still has some open areas. Until the Verranzano-Narrows Bridge opened in 1965, it was impossible to get from any other city location to the island except by boat. Since then, the open areas have become fewer and, as these become developed, brushfires will present less and less of a threat. However, if your area of protection, like Staten Island, is expanding into what was formerly woodlands or recreational land, you have a potentially demanding combination: a source of ignition (people) and nonstructural but fast-burning fuel (brush) now near structures. This situation usually arises in an area that is underserved by the fire service since historically there were no reasons to give it much attention. The results can be devastating, as they were in April 1963 when more than 100 homes were lost on Staten Island as several brushfires, fanned by high winds, merged into one large conflagration.

The obvious plant concern when it comes to natural disaster is to make sure that your building can withstand whatever is likely to occur. I was standing in the Turk Street Communications Center of the San Francisco Fire Department when a tremor shook the building. A dispatcher assured me that the facility was earthquakeproof "so far"! You'll also want to consider less obvious factors such as the flood plain. And if your protection district includes brushfire areas, besides taking the obvious measure of cutting down any brush that may be near your emergency communications center, your operation will probably be better equipped to deal with them if it has a meteorological instruments area. This is needed so that the "Spread Index" (a measure of the effect of weather on the relative rate of forward movement of surface fires) can be calculated. This calculation, based on a U.S. Forest Service formula, takes into account temperature, humidity, wind speed, precipitation in the past 24 hours, number of days since the last significant rainfall, and condition of vegetation (also referred to as the stage of herbal curation and classified as whether the vegetation is in a green, transitional, or cured state). The gathering of this data requires anemometers on your roof, wet and dry bulb thermometers, rain gauges, and the like. Your plant must have functional space for these items, as well as for any additional maps you may require if you use fire tower reports to triangulate "smokes" reported by tower watchmen.

LABOR DISPUTE

A labor dispute between communications personnel and management does not have to reach the walkout stage for your department's emergency communications operation to be affected. When FDNY firefighters went on a four-hour strike in November 1973, dispatchers found themselves in a vortex of conflicting emotions and loyalties. They were a dedicated group that was having difficulty believing that the firefighters had actually walked (it was later learned that their leader had misled them about a strike vote). Yet the dispatchers were also part of a city workforce that relied heavily on its union representatives to protect it from the possibility of poor upper management. The dispatchers had a positive attitude toward the delivery of service, but *they* were faced with the ringing phones when they had little service to deliver to the callers. Furthermore, there was the logistical and political problem of what to do about firefighters picketing the five borough central offices. Since at that time the dispatchers' tour of duty started at 8:00 a.m., they would have a fresh crew in place before any job action would commence at the start of the firefighters' day tour, 9:00 a.m. But what to do at 4:00 p.m.? If you crossed the picket lines, you divorced yourself from the much larger Uniformed Firefighters Association, whose support you might have needed someday. If you did not cross, then how were the people of New York supposed to survive? The dispatchers who were on duty for the day tour could reasonably be expected to work through to midnight—all of them had done 16-hour tours in the past. But after midnight, you were talking heavy fatigue time, not only from the long hours but also from the stress of the situation: trying to hold your thumb in the dike when it was likely that there were other holes breaking out that you didn't even know about; knowing that what field forces were working would be tired and possibly sabotaged; knowing that the hundreds of small fires which break out every day in the city would become much larger fires before anyone would be able to get to them (indeed, requests from field forces for more help were denied that day—"You'll have to hold it with what you've got!" was the general response).

Your plant concerns in such a situation are similar to those in a natural disaster—preparation for prolonged operations by the same personnel, but with one important additional consideration. Much as we find it repugnant even to think about it, we must deal with the possibility of sabotage if we are to prepare responsibly for functioning in a labor dispute. Critical areas at risk to sabotage must be identified. You may find it necessary to strengthen your facility's links to phone, electric, gas, and water utilities. If you have remote radio transmitters or receivers, the land lines to these installations must be secure or you will lose contact with your field forces. Some rural areas of the country that have shared transmitter facilities atop local mountains have had to deal with vandalism by thoughtless hikers. By evaluating your ability to withstand willful sabotage, you will also strengthen your position against all acts of terrorism, vandalism, and stupidity that could disrupt your operation.

NUCLEAR ACCIDENT

Fortunately, we don't have too much experience with this one. We have found out a lot from drills, however. I was in the Lacey (New Jersey) Township Emergency Operations Center to observe a nuclear disaster drill for the Oyster Creek nuclear power plant. Among the many lessons learned from the event was that a dispatcher's knowledge of both regional geography and meteorological instruments is important, given the potential for radioactive gases to vent into the air. It's also important to be familiar with the terminology: Such concepts as "wind dispersal pattern" and "exposure plume pathway" get thrown around fairly quickly during incident command decisions about population evacuations. In such an accident, plant location takes on significance; preferably your emergency communications center should not be situated such that prevailing winds would put it in a likely "at risk" position. But regardless of whether or not your geographical situation is safe in relation to wind patterns, you may wish to consider constructing a fallout shelter in which personnel could operate until a "hot" area cools off. In addition to maps of areas extending beyond your immediate jurisdiction, it is useful to have dedicated phone lines (so-called "hot" lines) to regional authorities such as county government, the state police, or even the state governor (who, presumably, would be the one to call out the National Guard) since the consequences of any nuclear accident are of a much larger scale than that on which any local emergency communications center operates.

OTHER "PEOPLE" CONCERNS

So far, we have been talking about matching your plant to the tasks that are to be performed in it and to the conditions under which those tasks are to be performed; and the people in it, specifically the personnel-oriented areas of safety, security, and crisis operations. There are a few other "people" items that should not be overlooked when planning the physical surroundings of your emergency communications operation:

Chairs. A dispatcher spends almost all of his time sitting down. Though emotionally it can be a roller coaster, physically it is a sedentary job. While there is always an argument over "comfort" versus "attention level," I cannot emphasize strongly enough the need for strong, comfortable chairs in the communications center.

Exercise. Precisely because of the sedentary nature of dispatching, an exercise area is a good investment for the department. "A sound mind in a healthy body" is not just an adage, and a sound mind is definitely needed to keep up with the mental demands of this job. Although to my knowledge there are no studies keyed specifically to communications personnel, there are numerous reports which show that when employers offer exercise programs or sponsor membership in health clubs, there is an increase in productivity and morale and a decrease in sick leave and injuries. In an emergency communications center, an exercise area has to be connected with the operations area by intercom to allow for the rapid recall of exercising personnel should conditions warrant. Of course, individual protocols for medical clearance, hours of use, and so forth are necessary. But if you have the space, you can lengthen the productive lives of your personnel by dedicating some of it to an exercise area.

Lighting. Although we will talk more about lighting and glare off CRT screens in Chapter Six, at this point I just want to alert planners to the effect of working in a high-stress position in fluorescent glare every day. Add to this the visual alarm indicators and the "Midnight Sun" effect of 24-hour operations and you begin to see the importance of planning your lighting with your people in mind. Remember that they may often work for 16 hours at a stretch. You may want to structure your lighting in operational segments so that only key areas are lit during night-time and early morning hours rather than having the whole place look like the Tower of Light, 24 hours a day. This protects against the "bunker" feeling by giving dispatchers an innate sense of the passage of time. It also saves money as well as eyesight!

Ergonomics. This is the name given to the applied science concerned with the characteristics of people that need to be considered when designing and arranging things they use. The objective is for people and things to "interact" effectively and safely. Whatever you do with your physical plant, keep in mind the *people* who will work there, often for long hours and under less-than-optimal conditions. When you have at least mentally "walked a mile in their shoes" you can be fairly confident that the outcome of your efforts will be productive and well-received.

And now, since we've been talking about tailoring so much of your physical plant to dispatchers, let's take a look at just who these people are.

CHAPTER TWO

Dispatchers

W E ASK THEM to work in what is essentially an unrecognized, low-profile job. We ask them to be the critical link—the lifeline—between the public and its protectors. We ask them to have a working expertise in a broad variety of subjects, from traffic patterns to harbor currents, from local ordinances to foreign languages, from hazardous materials to our own rules and regulations, and everything in between. We expect them to work any hours, any days, and to do so until relieved. We expect them to make on-the-spot, life-and-death decisions about the deployment of human resources and millions of dollars worth of equipment. We ask them to do work that may well interfere with their family life and also cause them to increase the amount of money they spend on antacids. We ask them to deal with the needy, the terrified, the angry, the lost, the drunken, the confused, the psychotic, the abusive, the lonely, and sometimes the dying people of our cities and towns. We ask them to direct field forces. And, generally, we don't pay them very well. In short, we want masochists with enough self-esteem to give direction!

Who *are* these people, and where do we find them? Job descriptions vary and usually do not pinpoint adequately the intangible "something" that makes a good dispatcher. That "something" is difficult to put into words. But most people in the field can tell you what they don't want in a dispatcher applicant—when you have had the experience of working with a "bad" dispatcher, it sticks with you. Here are some "don't wants":

The Genius. You don't want the person who thinks he is smarter than everybody. You know him: the one who fights the fire from the office; the one who second-guesses the paramedics all the time; the "I told you so" champ who will not let anybody forget mistakes. This guy is a morale buster who needs to build himself up by putting the knock on others. Curiously, the use of his powerful intellect is not limited to critiques of the performance of those around him. It also gets quite a workout when rationalizing his own failures—in fact, the only mistakes made in the communications center that this guy *can* forget are his own.

Napoleon. You don't want the person whose primary job satisfaction is derived from giving people orders. A dispatcher's focus is definitely in the wrong place when he says, "*I* am sending you to . . ." rather than "*You* are needed at . . ." I once worked with a guy who told me with undisguised pleasure, "You know, a battalion chief makes a lot more money than a dispatcher, but he's still gotta take orders from me." A good manager—one whose job necessarily includes giving orders—takes some pride from accomplishing his organization's goals through the motivation and direction of personnel. But he will frequently tell you that the actual giving of orders is the least rewarding part of his job. A dispatcher gives direction and advice. He is merely an agent of the authority that lies within the department, the county, the city, or whatever governmental body for which he is working (and, I might add, usually working within very clearly defined guidelines and expectations). A problem arises when Napoleon thinks that the authority is his. A more normal desire for Napoleon would not be "the joy of giving orders," but to close the salary gap between himself and the chief a little bit!

The Invisible Man. This fellow can disappear at the drop of an alarm. Need someone to do some tedious clerical work. . . street name updates, end-of-the-month statistics? He's gone! In the bathroom, out to lunch, in the parking lot, wherever—he's no-where to be seen. Need somebody to go out and buy lunch for the crew? Clean up the kitchen? Need a volunteer for overtime? Taking up a collection for a co-worker's new baby? You name it and The Invisible Man goes into his act. Worse, he also is adept at vanishing when the alarm rate begins to increase. He has his rationalizations for this behavior. "I've been here fifteen years—it's time for somebody else to do some work" (conveniently forgetting, of course, that there were earlier versions of this lament at every year from five on). In a job where folks spend a lot of stressful time with one another either through too much stimulation or not enough, having a weak link who will not share the load only makes it worse.

Mr. Show Biz. This is a fellow who would like to edit some of the old department tapes so he can produce "A Medley of My Greatest Alarms." He thinks that *he* is the reason people listen to scanners. He barks orders. He rolls his *r*'s like the old "Racket Squad" show. He resonates, he rhymes. In short, he performs. He can be a detriment to the overall operation in many ways. Concerned more about the frills of his on-air technique than with the performance of his job, this gent lets his ego get in the way of clear communications. He can also adversely affect the perform-ance of others by not letting them get enough on-air experience to sharpen their skills.

You see a lot of these folks and you sometimes wonder if they have limitless bladders, since they are often heard on the radio for hours and hours of heavy fire traffic. I knew one fellow who used to call his friends and tell them "I'm on." I have seen others who have skipped meals so they could stay on the radio. (Ob-viously, there is also question of poor supervision here as well.) While their understanding of the job may be adequate, they miss an essential point: Histrionics on the radio doesn't make it in the serious business of emergency communications.

The Politician. It's easy to spot this guy by the telephone that seems to be permanently attached to his ear. No, he is not so dedicated to the service that he continually answers fire phones. He is making "deals." He may be lobbying for his own promotion or seeking to have somebody else become indebted to him by arranging a transfer for them.

I knew a dispatcher who had a friend in headquarters. The friend used to see the transfer list before it came out and call the dispatcher. The dispatcher would then call one of the impending transferees and tell him that he (the dispatcher) "might just be able to swing a transfer" for the pigeon when he saw the deputy commissioner at a party that night. The dispatcher would go home and watch wrestling on TV (or maybe he actually would go to the same function as the deputy commissioner, but he wouldn't come within 25 feet of him unless he ran into him in the men's room!), the transfer would come through, the transferee would be eternally grateful, the dispatcher would get a thank-you bottle of scotch, and those who didn't know any better would be in awe of the dispatcher's "power."

The Politician makes others uneasy, not only because he doesn't do his share of the work, but also because he flaunts his "connections." If somebody notices that the fire extinguishers in the communications office need recharging, for example, The Politician won't bother to pick up a phone and ask the nearest company to stop by and pressurize the cans. No, that's too straightforward. Instead, The Politician will harrumph and make a show, saying, "The next time I see Councilman Whosis, he'll be very interested in *that*!" You have to be careful of the dispatcher applicant who is referred to you by the local pol. He may turn out to be an okay dispatcher. But he may turn out to be a large pain in the neck as well. Anyone who thinks he is exempt from the rules is a problem. Furthermore, study after study shows that the primary concern of workers in any setting is the sharing of information with the work force. Anytime somebody gives the impression that he has the inside track or has the ear of the higher-ups, your work force becomes that much more difficult to manage. More of their time is spent reacting to The Politician; more of your time is spent dealing with the problems this causes.

It's easy to recognize the kinds of people you don't need in your communications center, but painting a mental picture of your ideal dispatcher is anything but simple. Doing that—and finding people who'll best fit the picture—is the big management challenge.

JOB DESCRIPTION

Let's decide who the dispatcher is and how we go about finding him. We want to know what to put in our want ads. We want a job description.

There are many ways to attack the problem of settling on a job description. Depending on the complexity of the job and the political considerations of your setting such as a civil service system, you can get as simple or as complicated as you want. Usually, the starting point is a job analysis. This is a part of employment planning that clarifies certain aspects of a job. You'll want to look at both tangible and intangible aspects of the dispatcher's job, specifically identifying the knowledge, skills, experience, and personal qualities that you believe make for a good dispatcher. There are both objective and subjective angles to this identification process.

OBJECTIVE SCREENING CRITERIA

First, list very general, minimum-level skills that will constitute a screening threshold for candidates and will provide you with a very useful guideline for drafting a want ad. They will differ from area to area and from agency to agency, but here are some broad criteria:

• *Verbal Skills*. The successful candidate must demonstrate basic proficiency in English and any other language required in your area. After all, this is communications we're talking about! Whether or not the candidate meets this standard can be ascertained by testing or by interview. Testing is recommended for the initial screening and for larger operations because it's a more objective evaluation and demands less of your personnel office's time. At one time, a high school diploma was sufficient evidence that the standard was met. Unfortunately, this is no longer the case.

• *Writing Skills*. The successful candidate is able to transcribe telephone calls and radio reports to incident tickets (legibility, particularly with numbers, is very important here).

• *Typing Skills*. Typing becomes important if the information is to be recorded on a computer screen rather than an incident ticket. Since very few dispatchers ever went to secretarial school, it is safe to say that the two-finger method is okay here.

• *Good Health.* Some departments require only a medical exam, some a physical test. If you require that your dispatchers perform some specific physical activity that's outside the norm for a clerical position (such as climbing a ladder to the roof to collect weather data, starting an emergency generator with a pull rope, being certified in CPR, or using fire extinguishers and standpipes), stipulate that proof of the candidate's general good health, in the form of a physician's note, be submitted before he is allowed to take the physical test. Then give a test that is relevant to the work required. Unlike police officers or firefighters, dispatchers do not engage in many activities that make random sorts of physical demands on them. If there are any physical tasks at all, they are usually similar in nature to those described above. Therefore, duplicating the actual physical task to be performed is usually the best measure of suitability. It also eliminates any questions of relevance in testing.

• *Clean Criminal Record.* Given the sensitive nature of much of public safety communications work, in many cases a prior felony conviction eliminates a candidate from consideration. Misdemeanors should be evaluated individually for relevance and severity. If, for example, a misdemeanor charge was the result of a plea-bargain down from a felony, more thorough investigation is called for. A charge stemming from an isolated, less serious event (for example, noisily celebrating a basketball championship while still in high school) should still be examined for clues to some of the more subjective parts of candidate selection, such as attitude. It should not, though, be an exclusionary criterion by itself.

• *Drug Testing.* This is an extremely sensitive area in personnel management. Those who are concerned about the protection of civil liberties feel that drug testing is another way of saying "guilty until proven innocent." Others feel equally strongly that the sensitivity of the dispatcher's positon mandates that all possible safeguards be taken. You will have to read the political seas in your own area to make a decision on drug testing. However, no matter what position you take you should make it crystal clear from the outset that substance abuse on the job is intolerable.

If you opt for drug testing, it's better to schedule it further on in the selection process so that a number of candidates will have already been eliminated from consideration on the basis of other screening criteria. Thus you'll reduce not only testing fees but your exposure to controversy and its attendant costs.

Beyond these very general categories, the evaluation process takes on a more narrow focus. Other objective screening criteria should be pegged specifically to what you expect your communications personnel to actually *do* in the course of a shift. If in addition to dispatching you require them to perform municipal housekeeping chores such as receiving requests for pistol permits, processing the town's auto registrations, and issuing controlled burn permits, you may want to supply applicants with the regulations covering these tasks. Candidates will then have the opportunity to study them.

If you expect that your dispatchers be able to perform certain basic electrical operations such as line testing, fuse changing, and transferring feeder conductors in the terminal room, incorporate this into your job description. Also include this in your list of skills to be measured in your written test, should you give one.

SUBJECTIVE SCREENING CRITERIA

The transition from objective to subjective measurement criteria occurs when you include a standard such as "prior related experience." Consider what this means before putting it into your classified ad or position description. For one thing, prior related experience should be something that boosts a candidate's stock, not something whose absence excludes a candidate from consideration. "Prior related experience *preferred*" is the terminology—and the idea—that you're looking for. After all, how many young potential dispatchers in your labor market have actually done this kind of work before? You don't want to "specify yourself" out of the market. On the other hand, getting somebody with prior emergency communications experience can be a real plus to your operation.

What exactly should you consider to be related to actual emergency communications experience? How far do you go? A taxi dispatcher? An air traffic controller? A ham radio enthusiast? A switchboard operator? An electrician's apprentice?

Some years back, New York City's personnel folks decided that prior "public contact work" would be an acceptable gauge of suitability for the position of fire alarm dispatcher. Asked how he qualified to take the test, one youngster answered, "I worked the cash register in my uncle's restaurant!" Fortunately for FDNY, working the cash register of a Lower East Side restaurant can be fairly stressful and demanding, and the kid made a great dispatcher. It was also pointed out by the more cynical among the FDNY dispatching force that the "public contact work" yardstick would allow hookers to qualify for the exam rather easily! The moral of the story is to consider very carefully what you stipulate in your written standards.

After you struggle with the more subjective fringes of what constitutes related experience, focus on the desirable qualities of an emergency communications dispatcher. Consider in particular two components of the job analysis, job context and work performance, and their attendant questions. What is the work schedule? What are the physical working conditions? What are your standard error allowances? What is the permissible time taken for a particular task? How can you predict compatibility between a candidate and these kinds of conditions and benchmarks?

Make absolutely sure in your job analysis that you include *all* physical tasks that a dispatcher performs. Sometimes the tasks are either so routine as to escape notice or are seasonal (such as the gathering of weather information during the brushfire seasons in spring or autumn). This is another area in which outside consultation can be far more valuable than an in-house analysis. From his outside perspective, the consultant is more likely to look past the trees and see the forest. By neglecting to list all job tasks in the job context analysis, you not only risk hiring someone who is unqualified or unable to perform the necessary functions—you also risk litigation. I'm familiar with a case in which the relationship between job context (specifically, physical working conditions) and candidate testing was ignored. A physically impaired candidate met the written job requirements, performed well in objective testing, and after hiring proved to be a capable dispatcher—but he was unable to gain safe access to the emergency communications building. No one in management had chosen to exercise some realistic subjective judgment in the evaluation. The dispatcher's subsequent accidents and injuries led to a great deal of both administrative and personal heartache for all concerned. Fortunately, the size of the department involved was a plus, and a suitable working environment—one that afforded him safe access—was found for him.

Of course, the probationary employment period provides a built-in buffer for error in candidate selection. Most probationary periods are only ninety days, however, and even the most undesirable candidate can usually disguise his personal inadequacies for that period of time (although job performance errors, being more empirically measurable, are more difficult to hide). It is far easier to turn away a candidate than to remove a probationary employee. You may wish to consider having a longer probationary period and having "competency thresholds" in which the new dispatcher does not move on to the next phase of the probationary period until minimum competency has been clearly demonstrated in the earlier phases.

The bottom line on any subjective measurement of a candidate is "gut feeling." Depending on your municipality's employment system and how well you can manipulate it, there may not be room for gut feeling in candidate selection. There is good reason for this. The potential for abuse—nepotism, cronyism, discrimination—is very high. How does one legitimize "gut feeling"? One way is to make a letter of recommendation a requirement for candidates. It may not be appropriate to use your own instincts as a measuring stick, but that doesn't mean you can't draw on the feelings of others who are familiar with the candidate.

Some managers obtain a measure of the candidate by creating situations in the interview process and gauging a candidate's responses to them. Having a candidate wait for a long time past his scheduled interview or having him fill out application papers a second time because they have been "lost" by the secretary, for instance, is supposed to help measure disposition and frustration tolerance. In my opinion these artificial constructs are no substitute for a manager's good judgment.

JOB-RELATED QUESTIONS

The basis for judging a candidate's suitability can be broadened by presenting him with job-related situations to discuss. A series of hoops and hurdles aimed at tripping up the candidate is negative and more like a fraternity hazing than an employment screening process. Rather, give the candidate a chance to display his skills positively; this will give you a better read on his potential usefulness to your department.

A sharp emergency communications manager monitors his operation constantly for those "curve balls" that tax the creativity of his staff. He does this not only for postincident group critiques; he also stores them in his memory for use at interview time, for it's the difficult, challenging events that bring out the best in people. You certainly want to see the best your candidate has to offer, so base your questions on these real and demanding events. You might phrase your questions as such: "Recently, we were faced with a situation in which the first-arriving units at the scene of an underground construction collapse reported that they needed heavy shoring timbers to reach trapped workers. They also reported that a ruptured water main in the area was causing the excavation to fill with water. What would you, as the radio dispatcher, do in that case? What would you think about?"

You shouldn't expect a demonstrated familiarity with departmental procedure (FDNY, for example, has a standard litany of questions to ask when a company officer reports an apparatus accident) since the candidate is not yet a member of the department. What you should look for is creativity, flexibility, the ability to "think on your feet," and the talent to comprehend all parts of a problem, prioritize them, and use available resources to effect a solution. In the scenario above there are several key issues: The life hazard has not been fully defined. How many workers? Are they injured, unconscious, or could they participate in their own rescues? Is this an open trench or is lighting needed? How much shoring timber is needed and of what minimum size? Where can we get such timber and how can we get it to the scene? Is there some other event that has caused both the collapse of the excavation and the rupture of the water main? Or did one cause the other? Can the water main be shut off at some valve remote from the scene? Will underwater breathing apparatus buy time while the questions of holding back both rising water and falling earth are attacked?

Even though the officer in charge at the scene probably will be running these same questions through his own mind, anticipating them can help the dispatcher get an extra step ahead that can make the difference. And, although I am aware of one case in which a dispatcher was reprimanded by a superior for offering specific alternatives to an officer in charge at a fireground, two heads are almost always better than one. Asking certain questions might lead the field officer to consider some solutions that might not have occurred to him. Perhaps the dispatcher has handled a similar event before and the officer has not. In any case, you want to know how your candidate thinks. Does he see the larger picture? If you have a structural fire under a steel deck bridge, will he anticipate the need for another company (and perhaps another water source) to cool the bridge while the companies below work on the fire? Can he be helpful without being overbearing? Will he take pride in his own job or will he want to "fight the fire from the office"? Will he show the same degree of courtesy and attention to the little old lady with the cat in the tree as he will to the caller with the megadisaster?

How will the candidate deal with obnoxious callers and the "wackos"? I remember very clearly the night we informed an engine company officer that the rest of his first-alarm assignment would be delayed because of other alarm activity in his district. So the officer made an instantaneous judgment about the best way to attack a fire. He took his company into the rear of a burning six-story apartment building through the backyard of an adjoining private house on the next street over. The company got water on the fire, made three rescues, and performed a substantial amount of ventilating before the first truck company, special-called from a distance, arrived on the scene. Everyone was feeling pretty good about the rescues and the fine performance of the engine company when we received a complaint. "What are you going to do about my tomato plants?!" a man screamed at the answering dispatcher. The dispatcher thought for sure that the caller had a wrong number until the details of the complaint became known. The caller was the owner of the private house immediately behind the fire building. In their haste to save lives and property, those "inconsiderate firemen," without asking permission to use the yard, had gone "running right through in their big boots, dragging hose" and had trampled the caller's tomato plants. The dispatcher, normally somewhat jaded and cynical after years of dealing with the problems of society day after day, was still feeling a sense of pride over being part of the team that had accomplished three rescues. He tried to explain to the man the full significance of what had just happened. "After all, sir, the lives of three of your neighbors have just been saved. Surely, although we *are* sorry about your tomato plants, you understand that a greater good has been served here." Whereupon the irate and ignorant caller proceeded to inform the dispatcher that he didn't know anybody in that building, but he did know how much time and effort he had put into his garden; he was going to complain to his councilman, write a letter to the paper, and send the mayor a bill for the tomatoes! And he did! Besides knowing how to get the most appropriate help to people in the fastest possible time, your candidate will have to know how to deal with the overzealous backyard tomato gardeners of the world as well. Give him the opportunity to show that he does.

As your candidate responds to the situations you give him, you will get a feeling for his familiarity with your protection area, his fluency in the fire service, and his sense of himself and the way he sees the job for which he is applying. In presenting cases to test the candidate's reactions, be sure to leave out some details. In the flooding construction excavation incident noted before, the questions that immediately come to the mind of an experienced dispatcher arise from omitted specifics in the initial report. To see exactly how a good dispatcher wraps his mind around a particular problem, try your test cases out on your dispatching force before you use them in the interview process. In addition to getting some ideas about possible responses, it is also a good exercise for your troops.

STRESS

Make very sure your candidate understands that the dispatcher's position is extremely stressful. Find out what kind of stressors he anticipates. Ask what he does in his spare time, what his hobbies are, how he relaxes. Be a little concerned if all of his spare-time activities revolve around listening to the scanner. You want somebody who is dedicated to the service (and many good dispatchers get their initial interest from being "buffs"), but you don't want to hook up with somebody whose entire personality is going to be defined by the job. The well-rounded individual will have a steadier base from which to withstand job pressures.

Be sure to find out (either through the medical exam or by interview) if the candidate has a history of cardiac problems. Many larger police and fire departments assign their "light-duty" members to communications positions. This is fine if the injured party is recovering from a broken bone. If he is coming back from a heart attack, sending him to emergency communications can be like throwing a brick to a drowning man. A stress study conducted a few years ago by the Walter Reed Army Research Institute was done in the Montgomery County, Maryland Fire and Rescue Communications Center because the researchers felt that such a setting was "similar to strategic command center operations in a time of war."

Some job stressors are more obvious than others. For instance, the dispatcher cannot stay home if it snows. Nor can he leave work at the end of his shift unless somebody else comes in to relieve him. Unlike a factory or an office job, the dispatcher's work—and having him there to do that work—is essential to public safety. The dispatcher works on weekends and holidays, but the stressful "24 hours, 365 days" nature of the work has less obvious manifestations. One is the stress that comes with working different shifts, particularly at night. You cannot overlook the influence of natural body rhythms on performance. Some people, despite all the best intentions, simply and truly cannot function at night. They cannot sit down and eat a meal at three-thirty in the morning, and, no matter how much sleep they may have gotten prior to coming to work, at dawn their legs always feel like Silly Putty. The effects of what are known as circadian cycles—the regular metabolic, glandular, and sleep rhythms and behavioral patterns associated with the 24-hour cycle of the earth's rotation—are well known in the medical world. A computer search of recent medical literature on the subject turned up ten full pages of references, yet public safety providers do not pay all that much attention to it. While some folks may be primarily nocturnal and others dominantly diurnal, you want your dispatcher to be able to function optimally at any time. We will speak more of some of the ways in which your department can respond to this concern in Chapter Three, "Scheduling Dispatchers."

A less obvious consequence of "always being there" is the stress that comes with having a home away from home. More so than in most other work settings, dispatchers live together with their fellow workers. They eat together, sleep together, watch TV together. Furthermore, because the odd working hours tend to isolate them socially from the rest of the world—the "nine-to-fivers"—they quite frequently socialize together as well. Your dispatcher will have a much better chance of successfully functioning in your organization if he is able to get along with the people already working there. This does not imply that you must have the same type of people working in your communications center—far from it. It does mean that you need somebody who can get along with all the *different* types of folks who will be dispatching for you. Your candidate needs flexibility and adaptability, personally as well as professionally. A good background check will usually turn up any deficits in this area.

CIVILIAN OR UNIFORMED PERSONNEL?

Before getting into the controversy that occurs in some jurisdictions over the relative merits of using civilian dispatchers or uniformed communications personnel, decide what in your area constitutes the difference between the two. In some cases the difference is defined by a political delineation, with pay guidelines, benefits packages, and certain other benefits—most notably retirement thresholds and the so-called "heart provisions," which presume heart attacks suffered by any uniformed person to be job-related—drawing up the lines. In other cases, there is a question of status involved. In most departments, "uniformed" means being a member of the police department or fire department.

There are some obvious drawbacks to staffing your emergency communications operation solely with uniformed personnel. For one thing, it excludes a great many candidates who may make excellent dispatchers but do not meet entry level requirements for police officer or firefighter. Secondly, uniformed personnel in communications frequently "rotate through" the communications division rather than becoming career communications professionals. Career professionals provide desirable continuity and planning capability. Finally, uniformed personnel are more bound by the rank structure of the paramilitary organization, and this can get in the way in emergency communications. It is conceivable that a firefighter would feel somewhat uncomfortable giving orders over the radio to a captain (or perhaps *too* comfortable!). A civilian is outside that chain of command and less likely to run into any difficulties along those lines.

The area of field communications/mobile command post personnel often brings the "uniformed versus civilian" question to the fore. Personnel in this sector who are clearly designated in your Table of Organization as being within the communications division (as differentiated from being shown as part of the fire-fighting forces) are subject to the same personnel guidelines as anyone else in your division; however, in cases where the department plans to use civilian dispatchers to staff its mobile command post (usually contemplated as a cost-saving measure because, unfortunately, dispatchers are paid far less than firefighters), there are personnel management considerations to take into account. In some jurisdictions the "outside" work assignment gives rise to liability, insurance, and pension concerns. Although emergency communications work is extremely stressful in many circumstances, it is often hard to make a case that it can be considered physical labor. In at least one civil service system of which I'm familiar, civilian eligibility for pension after twenty years of service depends on whether or not the job description meets the standard of "physically taxing" labor. Consequently, before assigning previously "inside" staff to "outside" duties, you would do well to check with counsel. There's no sense in opening a can of worms that will drain your time and funds in litigation or cause you to incur continuing liability for the cost of earlier-than-anticipated retirements.

Although it's embarrassing to talk about it, the second consideration with regard to civilian dispatching personnel in mobile command posts is how well they will handle the additional responsibilities. The fact is that some dispatchers are frustrated firefighters or cops. Some people get crazy when you put them behind the wheel of a car that has lights and sirens on it! This may sound bizarre to those of you who do not have firsthand operational experience with emergency communications, but—trust me—I have seen it many times in many places. If you are fortunate, this won't be something you'll have to consider. But remember that once you start a practice, you live with it. You may have steady and mature personnel now, but that doesn't mean that you'll always have them.

Your ability to establish clearly defined hiring standards and practice effective hiring procedures, how many and which candidates you choose, and how you use these people—specifically, how they are scheduled to work—will have a great impact on every part of your department's operation. In the next chapter, we will look at the far-ranging effects of work schedules for a 24-hour emergency communications service.

CHAPTER THREE

Scheduling Dispatchers

EVERYBODY KNOWS THAT the fire department is always there, 24 hours a day, seven days a week, 365 days a year—when you call, they answer. What does it take to have someone answering that fire phone all year? I'd bet that most civilians, if asked that question, would talk about hiring people to work three shifts and pretty much let it go at that. Those of us in the business know better. The scheduling of emergency communications personnel is a complex and changing problem, influenced today by factors not even considered just a few years ago.

Staffing and scheduling decisions for emergency communications personnel should take many factors into account. In the last chapter we looked at who we wanted to fill our positions. Now, we will look at both "how many" and "how."

STAFF SIZE

How many? is not an easy question to answer. The National Fire Protection Association's *NFPA 1221: Standard for the Installation, Maintenance and Use of Public Fire Service Communication Systems* gives you some beginning guidelines. It recommends that jurisdictions receiving between 600 and 2,500

---

alarms annually have at least one dispatcher "especially trained for the service" on duty at all times, and at least two such dispatchers for more than 2,500 annual alarms. What it does not tell you are the ways to figure out how to get those "especially trained" bodies into your communications center.

Employment planning is a vast and intricate part of personnel management that includes technological forecasts (will you need more or fewer staff in a CAD system?), economic forecasts (if the seers predict the construction of thousands of new homes in your city, you had better be ready to protect them and their occupants), human resource supply and demand, retirement planning, attrition rates, recruitment, overtime, and wage and salary issues (if you pay less than the local fast-food chain, doesn't it stand to reason that, first, anybody with half a brain will go and flip hamburgers rather than work around the clock with the pressure of life-and-death decisions; and second, the people who you *will* get to be dispatchers for your department—if they are not independently wealthy and doing this for a hobby—might be less than the best possible candidates?).

To answer How many? you must break the question into two parts: (a) What's the minimum number of dispatchers required to run your dispatch center at any given time? and (b) How many bodies does it take to fill each of the positions arrived at in (a), 24 hours a day, every day of the year?

Obtaining the answer to (a) should be relatively easy. Note that the question asks about the *minimum* number of dispatchers needed. We are talking about routine operations here. You can always staff up for special events such as Fourth of July, Halloween, floods, brushfire season, and so forth. You can also use tactical scheduling in response to peak demand times.

Assess the number of seats you need to fill to cope with demand for service. If your department is a rural operation and receives 125 calls for help annually, almost none of them simultaneously, then your answer to (a) is one. If you have a larger area of protection, then you have to look at how the work breaks down. Do you segregate alarm receipt function from radio function? Is it impossible for the person doing the paperwork (or the computer updating) to keep track of the current status of unit availability and neighborhood protecton as well? Do you receive so many calls per hour that you need more than one person whose function is simply to receive calls? Do you have a voice communication system to firehouses (public address or voice alarm) that is separate from the radio with which you reach the field units?

When you have sufficiently analyzed the basic questions, then you will have your answer to (a). Usually there are fewer than five seats to fill in all but the largest city operations, where dozens of dispatchers work around the clock.

How do you figure out (b)? What is (b) all about, anyway? Simply put, there is a difference between determining how many seats need to be filled and how many bodies it takes to fill those seats. Your staffing needs are expressed in terms of full-time equivalencies (FTEs). An FTE is equal to the number of hours in your standard work week.

To determine FTE staffing requirements, figure out how many *productive* dispatcher hours you need to run your operation safely. For example, if you feel that you need two dispatchers on duty at all times, then you need two dispatchers times 168 hours in a week for a total of 336 dispatcher hours weekly, or 17,472 productive dispatcher hours annually (see Figure 3-1 on page 44). To calculate how many people must be hired to produce that many hours, start with whatever is your standard work week—in our example, we'll use 40 hours—and multiply by 52 weeks. From this total, subtract the nonproductive dispatcher hours. These are any paid hours for which the employee does not actually show up and work at his position, including vacation leave, holiday time, sick leave, and any training time you may require. For example:

Vacation leave (average 12 days annually) = 96 hours
Holiday time (average 8 days annually) = 64 hours
Sick leave (average 6.5 days annually) = 52 hours
Training time (1 day annually) = 8 hours

Total nonproductive hours = 220

In the 40-hours-per-week scenario, the 220 nonproductive hours subtracted from the total of 2,080 possible working hours per employee leaves you with a reasonable expectation of 1,860 productive dispatcher hours per employee annually. In our example, you know that you need 17,472 hours to run two dispatchers 24 hours a day, so you divide this number by the productive hours available from each employee: 17,472 / 1,860 = 9.39. This number does not necessarily mean that you need 9.39 people to do the job. What you need are 9.39 FTEs. How you divide those FTEs depends on several factors. Two 20-hour part-timers, for instance, could possibly share an FTE; each would be listed as a .5 FTE.

Figure 3-1
DETERMINING PRODUCTIVE HOURS NEEDED

24 hours per day × 7 days per week = 168 hours per week

168 hours per week × 2 chairs filled by dispatchers needed at all times = 336 productive dispatcher hours needed per week

336 productive dispatcher hours needed per week × 52 weeks per year = 17,472 productive dispatcher hours needed annually

It is important to remember that FTEs refer to hours and not people. You might be fortunate enough, for instance, to have some folks who work weekends only. You could staff your entire weekend with two different dispatchers a shift—six people—and use only 2.4 FTEs because, no matter how many *people* you have working during that time, you still have used only 96 dispatcher *hours* (see Figure 3-2).

Figure 3-2
THE DIFFERENCE BETWEEN NUMBER OF PERSONNEL AND NUMBER OF FULL-TIME EQUIVALENCIES (FTEs)

Shift	Saturday	Sunday
12–8 Ralph	8	8
Sue	8	8
8–4 Fred	8	8
Gerry	8	8
4–12 Randy	8	8
Mike	8	8
	48 +	48 =
	96 dispatcher hours	

$$\frac{96 \text{ hours needed}}{40 \text{ hours per FTE}} = 2.4 \text{ FTEs}$$

Although 6 different dispatchers cover the weekend, they use up only 96 hours of payroll rime, or 2.4 FTEs

Note that we have used eight-hour days to calculate non-productive time. And when we spoke of part-timers, we said that each might work 20 hours weekly, which obviously does not fit into an eight-hour-day structure. The fact is, when it comes to work, most budget processes, union contracts, and people's thinking are expressed in standard eight-hour days. However, there is not much standard about the hours kept by emergency service providers. Therefore, you must constantly adjust your thinking back and forth between the theory of "the rest of the world"—the "nine-to-five with weekends and holidays off" crowd—and the practice of your department's responsibilities.

Furthermore, you must think in terms of larger chunks of time. Sure, a .5 FTE is scheduled for 20 hours a week, and that doesn't fit into eight-hour shifts. But the same .5 FTE works 40 hours in *two weeks,* and that does fit into eight-hour shifts: three shifts one week and two the next. A little later, you'll be asked to alter your thinking again and break out of the eight-hour mold. But first, in further consideration of "how many," let's look again at the previous example in which we need 9.39 FTEs to staff our communications center with two dispatchers at all times.

Suppose we were dealing with a union contract or a county policy that did not allow for part-time workers. Would you hire nine dispatchers or ten? It's pretty close to ten anyway, so why not go for it? One of the reasons not to go for it is the cost of a full-time employee in addition to salary. Benefits for a full-timer generally cost around 30 percent of salary, with paid time off, insurance (especially health insurance), and pensions taking up the bulk of these expenses. One of the options to consider before hiring the tenth full-time dispatcher is to cover the tenth slot with overtime hours from the other nine employees. From a strictly numbers perspective, we see that to cover the additional .39 FTE there is an average of 16 hours to be worked weekly by the nine dispatchers (40 hours $\times$ .39 = 15.6 hours). This looks like a little more than 1.5 hours per dispatcher per week. The 16 hours paid at time-and-a-half work out to 24 hours of regular pay. The cost of benefits for a full-time employee (30 percent over salary) is equivalent to 52 hours of pay (40 hours × 130% = 52 hours). At first blush, it appears that you would do better to cover the additional .39 FTE with overtime, saving yourself 28 hours weekly, or 1,456 hours of pay annually.

But let's look at this again. Remember, this is not an office where everybody works next to everybody else for eight hours, then the doors close, the lights go out, and everybody goes home. Your doors never close. Your lights are always on. The assumption that you simply would be able to distribute the extra .39 FTE among the other nine workers defies the logistics of the situation. For one thing, can you predict exactly where the manpower shortfall will occur? Will it happen on the day shift? At night? At the same time each week? Will it always occur when you have personnel available to work the overtime? If not, you're facing a lot of problems. Do you want to get into the practice of ordering routine overtime? Beyond that, suppose the weekly gap in coverage is contingent to somebody's vacation or sick leave. After all, your nine other employees are going to average 166.5 days (9 employees × [12 vacation days + 6.5 sick days]) of such leaves annually. Then you would find yourself with 16 hours to cover. Finally, disbursements for some pension systems are based on the employee's earnings during his last year of service. Therefore, your estimate of the cost of that benefit has to be adjusted upward for overtime worked by those employees who are or are soon to be eligible for retirement. That upward adjustment takes the cost of covering with overtime far beyond the cost of a new hire.

So where is the cutoff? Like so many other related questions, the answer is "It depends." But at least this discussion will give you some idea of what it is that you, as a manager, should examine. In many cases, the emergency communications manager has resources at his disposal—the city actuary or county accountant or the personnel department's benefits manager, for instance—but simply does not know what questions to ask. For each situation, depending on a host of local issues (contract, ratio of benefits to salary, average of productive hours per employee, and so forth), there is a point of diminishing returns, both financial and logistical, on the question of hiring versus overtime. Have your local number crunchers figure out that point for you. Then decide if you want to adjust it even more by giving some weight to factors that do not readily show up on a balance sheet, such as low morale, burn-out, and tuning out to service demand. Their thresholds are lowered when communications center management adopts a policy of long-term overtime (exclusive of overtime for those periods that historically have required it, such as brushfire season). Increased sick leave, on-the-job injuries, poor decisions, and time lost to family concerns are the result. In the case we have been discussing (9.39 FTEs), hire the tenth dispatcher. The absolute worst that can happen as a direct result of such a hire would be that on some days you might have three dispatchers working in your communications center instead of two.

USING WHAT YOU'VE GOT

Running concurrently to your determination of the number of dispatchers on your staff is how to use them—you must predict fluctuating service demand. There are many ways to approach this problem, depending on your area of service. You can use the Spread Index to forecast brushfires. If yours is a seasonal resort area you should be attuned to population changes that will cause fluctuations in service demand. But the best way is to collect communications center data over an extended period of time and see what your experience has been. Since your department is already logging various times—receipt of alarm, arrival at the scene, return to quarters, and so forth—you should be able to collect retrospective service demand data fairly easily. After you have the numbers, plot them out on graphs. You should examine alarm incidence as a function of time of day and, perhaps, distribution of alarms by month (see Figure 3-3 on page 50). You may think that this represents the obvious, but sometimes the results are unexpected—and it's by exploring the unexpected results that you fine-tune your needs and get a better picture of your service demands.

After you have plotted the data, look for spikes and trends in the graph. If, for instance, you find that requests for service remain relatively constant from 2 a.m. until 6 p.m. but swing higher in the evening hours, you may want to staff up during the evening. The easiest way to do this is to schedule overlapping shifts. Consider yourself lucky if

1) your high-demand times are roughly concentrated in one block of hours. If you have what the statisticians call a "bimodal distribution" (that is, for example, you have one busy period in the evening and another in the early morning), you will not be able to cover these upswings with a single shift person;

2) your union contract allows you to schedule people creatively;

3) you can find a qualified person who wants to work from 6 p.m. until 2 a.m.; and

4) you can create a dispatchers schedule that will not violate the provisions of the Fair Labor Standards Act and/or cost you a lot of mandated overtime.

You or your counsel should be familiar with the applicable provisions of the Fair Labor Standards Act (FLSA) before you set out to alter any work schedules. The FLSA, passed by Congress in 1938, mandates that employees who work more than 40 hours in a week must be compensated for the excess time at the rate of one-and-a-half times their normal pay—popularly known as "time-and-a-half." When the FLSA was passed, however, it specifically excluded political subdivisions from its coverage. Beginning in 1961, a series of amendments gradually expanded the FLSA coverage, and an FLSA amendment in 1974 included most public employees under its aegis. A subsequent

Figure 3-3
ALARM INCIDENCE GRAPH

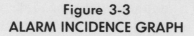

DISTRIBUTION OF ALARM BY TIME OF DAY

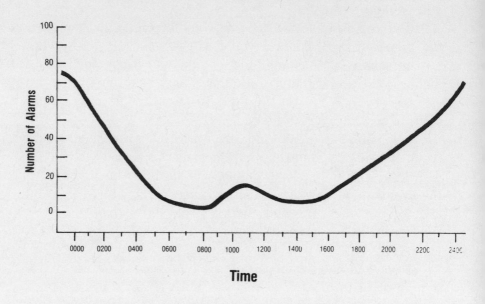

DISTRIBUTION OF ALARMS BY MONTH

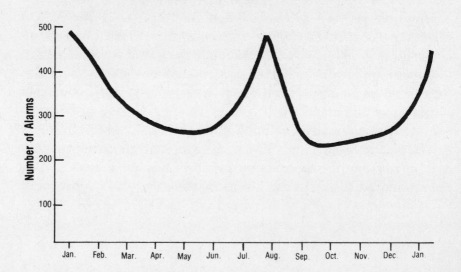

Supreme Court case (National League of Cities v. Usury, 426 U.S. 833, 1976) struck down the application of FLSA to state and local governments. However, only nine years later the court reversed its position. In February 1985, a Supreme Court decision (Garcia v. San Antonio Metropolitan Transit Authority, 469 U.S. 528, 1985) caused an outcry from public sector employers by requiring both time-and-a-half pay for hours in excess of 40 weekly and a ban on using compensatory time in lieu of pay for these excess hours. Local government officials claimed that this ban would destroy their budgets. Congress heard the complaints and, in April 1985, passed the Fair Labor Standards Amendments of 1985.

The 1985 amendments provide special rules for firefighters and police regarding work hours. These rules allow for the establishment of a work period longer than the usually accepted seven-day week for the purposes of computing overtime pay. (Exempt from overtime under the FLSA are firefighters and law enforcement personnel employed by public agencies with fewer than five employees.) Overtime payment for firefighters begins when they work more than 212 hours in a 28-day period. Departments whose work charts have fewer than 28 days must figure out their overtime thresholds proportionally from the 28-day ratio.

Emergency communications managers should note that subsequently to the 1985 FLSA amendments, the Wage and Hour Division of the U.S. Department of Labor has proposed new rules and regulations for public fire and police personnel (*Federal Register*/ Vol. 51/ No. 80/ Friday, April 25, 1986). Of particular interest is Section 553.210 (c), which states, "Not included in the term 'employee in fire protection activities' are the so-called 'civilian' employees of a fire department, fire district, or forestry service who engage in such support activities as those performed by dispatchers, alarm operators, apparatus and equipment repair and maintenance workers, camp cooks, clerks, stenographers. . . ."

While many emergency communications personnel will bristle at the very idea that they are lumped together with clerks and cooks, the fact is that there has been less leeway allowed management in dispatcher scheduling than in firefighter scheduling. If your operation is one of the many that assigns "light duty" uniformed personnel to communications, you should know that such situations were covered under the old rules. These firefighters were officially considered to be involved in fire protection activities even though assigned to support activities—that is, as stated in the *Federal Register,* "whether or not such assignment is for training or familiarization purposes, or for reasons of illness, injury, or infirmity."

All emergency communications managers are advised to either become familiar with the "Federal Rules and Regulations" promulgated by the Wage and Hour Division or to make sure that somebody in your department is. This division of the U.S. Department of Labor regulates such issues as sleeping and meal time, mutual aid, employees trading assigned work times between themselves, and early relief—all very much a part of the customs of the fire service. Making the wrong move here in the name of tradition can prove costly in light of modern regulations.

Some *basic* points to consider under FLSA:

• Compensatory time received by an employee in lieu of cash must be at the premium rate of not less than one-and-a-half hours of comp time for each hour of overtime work—the same as the calculation for cash payment.

• If the employee is engaged in an "emergency response activity"—which the regulations stipulate includes "dispatching of emergency vehicles and personnel" (Sect. 553.24 [c]—the maximum amount of comp time he can accrue is 480 hours. This represents time accrued for 320 hours of overtime work, or 40 overtime days at eight hours per day.

• The provisions of the regulations are in effect after April 15, 1986. This date is the starting point for the calculation of maximum accrual levels noted above.

Assuming that you have covered all the legal bases and understand any prohibitions you may face and the limitations within which you must work, you then can begin to look at actual schedules.

SCHEDULE TYPES: PROS AND CONS

The two basic categories of work schedules with which most members of the fire service are familiar are <u>rotating shifts,</u> which call for all members to work all hours of the day and night at some time, and <u>fixed shifts,</u> in which members always work set hours—"straight" days, evenings, or nights.

There are a variety of ways to fit your personnel into the hours of the day. Usually, a dispatcher is assigned to a group or a "platoon" whose schedule is plotted out on a work chart. The manager with part-time dispatchers on staff has great flexibility in scheduling weekends, vacations, and days off. If all your personnel are full-time employees, you may find that the easiest way to cover weekends and holidays is with a repeating cycle. The cyclical work schedule can be either rotating or straight.

You probably know by now that this is not simply a matter of plugging people into holes. When scientists write articles like "Apparent Phase-Shifts of Circadian Rhythms (Masking Effects) During Rapid Shift Rotation" and "Rotating Shift Work Schedules That Disrupt Sleep Are Improved by Applying Circadian Principles," you have to know that there is a lot more to it than that!

I'm going to tell you the story of the evolution of my favorite work schedule—the two-platoon, 25-day cycle, 25-group system—to demonstrate both how hard it is to come up with an effective scheduling system and the considerable number of unforeseen consequences, both good and bad, that arise out of a work schedule.

A few years back, FDNY dispatchers were on a schedule that required them to work two day tours (8 a.m. to 4 p.m.) followed by two evening tours (4 p.m. to 12 midnight) followed by two night tours (12 midnight to 8 a.m.). After this marathon, the dispatcher was entitled to 96 hours off duty. The entire cycle was worked by five groups and took ten days to complete (see Figure 3-4). One problem that confronted FDNY managers was immediately apparent: Six eight-hour shifts totaled only 48 hours in ten days. Since the dispatchers were classified in a labor group that worked a 37.5-hour week, they wound up short about four hours with this work configuration. (After six tours on three different shifts, I'm sure they didn't *feel* short of work, but mathematically they were!) In order to get the approximate ratio of 37.5 hours worked in a seven-day week (once again, the powers that be tend to figure things in terms of eight-hour days, with a half-hour for lunch, Monday to Friday, with weekends at the beach!), it was determined that the dispatchers needed to work 52 hours in the ten-day cycle.

Now, there just wasn't any easy way to plug these extra four hours into the work chart. What management decided was this: Each of the five dispatcher groups was split in half. On the first of the group's two day tours, half the dispatchers worked until 8 p.m., overlapping with the evening shift for four hours. On the second day tour, the other half of the group did likewise. The division managers went home at 4 p.m. So guess what happened. There were some terrific four-hour card games. Some four-star meals were prepared. A lot of college homework got done. But very few fire engines were dispatched any quicker. Why? Because the dispatchers were essentially lazy? Because they were trying to beat the system? Well, for some people, I'm sure these were influencing factors. But not for more than 200 dispatchers! In some cases, the reason why this went on was that there simply weren't enough workstations for the dispatchers. Sometimes, there weren't enough *chairs*! But the most basic and most significant reasons why the "extra four" program didn't work were two: an unwieldly system and weak supervision.

Figure 3-4
THREE-PLATOON, FIVE-GROUP CHART

Jan. 31 April 30 May 31	Feb. 28 June 30 July 31	March 31	12-8	8-4	4-12	Aug. 31	Sept. 30 Oct. 31	Nov. 30 Dec. 31
1-11-21-31	10-20-30	2-12-22	4	2	1	9-19-29	8-18-28	7-17-27
2-12-22	1-11-21-31	3-13-23	5	2	1	10-20-30	9-19-29	8-18-28
3-13-23	2-12-22	4-14-24	5	3	2	1-11-21-31	10-20-30	9-19-29
4-14-24	3-13-23	5-15-25	1	3	2	2-12-22	1-11-21-31	10-20-30
5-15-25	4-14-24	6-16-26	1	4	3	3-13-23	2-12-22	1-11-21-31
6-16-26	5-15-25	7-17-27	2	4	3	4-14-24	3-13-23	2-12-22
7-17-27	6-16-26	8-18-28	2	5	4	5-15-25	4-14-24	3-13-23
8-18-28	7-17-27	9-19-29	3	5	4	6-16-26	5-15-25	4-14-24
9-19-29	8-18-28	10-20-30	3	1	5	7-17-27	6-16-26	5-15-25
10-20-30	9-19-29	1-11-21-31	4	1	5	8-18-28	7-17-27	6-16-26

The "extra four" scheduling system was not demand-driven—that is, powered by the demands for fire protection service and by the needs of the people in the system. It was driven by a bureaucratic need that tried to place a square peg in a round hole. The dispatchers working in the system knew that it was structured this way simply to keep some accountant happy at the Office of Municipal Labor Relations. The department had to show that these employees were "on duty" for the correct number of hours, which would show them to be roughly (*very* roughly) congruent with other city workers in the same labor grade. That the dispatchers should become cynical was entirely predictable. Here was delivery of literally a life-and-death service being contorted in such a way as to pay lip service to the number crunchers. If the people in the system don't have respect for it, it's not going to work. In this case, it was apparent that the system and its devisers had no respect for the people in it or the work they did; the people in the system, the dispatchers, returned the sentiment. If the scheduling system had been demand-driven, it would have resulted in far greater productivity.

The issue of weak supervision had a couple of dimensions to it. One was that the managers went home at 4 p.m. Another was that the line supervisors, the supervising fire alarm dispatchers, were represented by the same union as the workers they supervised! For me, as the president of that union, it was a super deal. From a managerial standpoint, however, it was just plain dumb!

In any case, after years of wasted man-hours resulted from this system, an opportunity arose to change it. It is noteworthy that the impetus to change the scheduling system came from the dispatchers rather than from the communications division managers and was *originally* powered by economics. Simply put, the dispatchers wanted more money. They were the busiest fire alarm dispatchers in the world and among the lowest paid. Although the city would not say so publicly, its own comparative research supported the dispatchers' position. The key was how to find a way to pay the dispatchers considerably more money without causing an outcry from other municipal employees who would want to have a similar percentage increase. One face-saving solution was to announce that, yes, the dispatchers were going to be paid a lot more money, but they were all going to be working a lot more hours. The question then became how to structure those hours. Both sides knew that the current system was not working. The city wanted greater productivity and the dispatchers, even though they may not have articulated it as such at the time, wanted self-esteem. They wanted respect. They did *not* want to be paid for sitting around, doing nothing for four additional hours every other day tour. They felt that particular institutional stupidity to be personally demeaning.

The city's firefighters worked a schedule that some dispatchers thought was attractive but required modifications to suit their needs. It was a two-platoon, 25-day cycle, 25-group system. The firefighters' day shifts ran from 9 a.m. to 6 p.m., which seemed okay to the dispatchers; the 6 p.m. to 9 a.m. night shift, however, was just too much. Firefighters had down time between alarms, with the housewatch duty spread among all the company members. The dispatchers had a more constant service demand to deal with. Also, the firefighters could spend their down time in bunks, while dispatchers officially were not permitted to sleep in the communications center. So the dispatchers played around with the charts until they came up with the idea of all 12-hour shifts. The preferred shift-change times were at 7 a.m. and 7 p.m. The individual dispatcher would start his 25-day cycle on the first of two day shifts. He would work 7 a.m. to 7 p.m., be off for 12 hours, then come back and do it again. After completing his second day shift, he would be off for 24 hours, then return to duty on the third day of his cycle at 7 p.m. for the first of two night shifts: 7 p.m. to 7 a.m. with 12 hours off in between. After this he'd have a 96-hour "swing" in which he'd be off duty. He would return and repeat this cycle: two days on, two nights on, four days off. The third time around in the cycle, he would have a 120-hour swing at the conclusion of his last night shift (see Figure 3-5 on pages 60 and 61). It sounds confusing, but look at the illustrations and lay the schedule out on a calendar—you'll see that it can be the most attractive of any rotating schedule.

There are a lot of positive features to this system. At the time, of course, it provided a way for the FDNY dispatchers to work more hours—going from 37.5 to 40.32 hours weekly, an increase of almost eight percent—while making fewer appearances. But the strongest plusses were primarily unanticipated.

Fewer Appearances. Most people appear at work for five days out of every seven, or 71 percent of the time. The FDNY dispatchers, in their old counterproductive schedule, appeared six days out of 10 for a 60-percent appearance rate. By extending their working tour to 12 hours, dispatchers further reduced their number of required appearances to only 12 days out of every 25—a 48-percent required appearance rate. The dispatchers were appearing fewer times but staying longer when they did appear.

What does fewer appearances mean? For one thing, it decreases the number of trips to work that each individual dispatcher makes, thus decreasing traveling time and expenses. (At the time this schedule was being prepared for presentation to the city, we sought to have the New York State Department of Energy sanction it as a means of reducing fuel consumption.)

Another obvious advantage of making fewer appearances at work is that you have longer stretches of personal time. You also work fewer weekends. When you are scheduled to work a weekend, you spend more time on duty that particular weekend, but you actually have to show up for fewer weekends.

Furthermore, fewer appearances means reduction in the use of sick leave. Of course, if you look at the numbers, you'll see that it's mathematically self-evident: If you are scheduled to appear at work only 48 percent of the time (and this figure refers to the calendar days on which your assigned group is scheduled on duty; the appearance percentage decreases further when you factor in holidays and vacations), it stands to reason that the statistical likelihood of the random occurrence of illness is for you to be sick on one of your days off (more than half the time) rather than an on-duty day. If somebody calls in sick, he is charged with a full 12 hours of sick time for the tour missed. But from a managerial perspective it becomes easier to fill the sick worker's slot because the pool of personnel available for overtime is larger. Only 20 percent of your work force is on duty on any given shift—40 percent on any given day. The balance, therefore, is available for extra work.

Finally, by compressing more working hours into fewer appearances, members have more contingent time off. Under this schedule, each individual dispatcher is off duty for two four-day stretches and one five-day stretch every 25 days! Besides affording him the needed recharging time of 42 mini-leaves every year, it also enables him to get more mileage out of his vacation time (see Figure 3-6 on pages 62 and 63). If a dispatcher takes off the four days prior to his 120-hour swing and the four days after it, he uses 96 hours of leave but is away from his job for three weeks. Under a five-day system, in order to get three weeks off you have to use 120 hours of leave time.

Timing of Shift Changes. When the dispatchers moved the start of their day tours from 8 a.m. to 7 a.m. there was some grumbling about getting up earlier in the morning. Nonetheless, after a few months people realized that because they left home earlier and avoided the morning rush hour, their travel time was decreased. This also led to further fuel savings, but, more importantly, a big reduction in commuter stress.

Under the three-platoon system at FDNY, evening dispatchers came on duty at 4 p.m., meaning they left for work before the kids got home from school. They finished work at midnight, fairly wound up from their tour of duty, to come home to a house where everybody was asleep. Frequently, the preferred alternative was to "unwind with the boys" at a local watering hole before going home to a dark, quiet house. This led to higher opportunistic alcohol abuse, to DWI accidents and the sick leave that went with them, to fights in bars, and to getting

Figure 3-5
TWO-PLATOON, 25-GROUP, 25-DAY CYCLE

cycle days	Jan. July	Feb. July	Mar. Dec.	Apr. May.	May.	June	Aug.	Sept.	Oct. Nov.	Nov.	ON DUTY 7 a.m. to 7 p.m.	ON DUTY 7 p.m. to 7 a.m.	cycle days
1	21	15	12	6	1 26	20	9	3 28	23	17	22 23 24 25 1 2	16 17 (18) 19 20 21	1
2	22	16	13	7	2 27	21	10	4 29	24	18	25 1 2 3 4 5	19 20 (21) 22 23 24	2
3	23	17	14	8	3 28	22	11	5 30	25	19	3 4 5 6 7 8	22 23 (24) 25 1 2	3
4	24	18	15	9	4 29	23	12	6	1 26	20	6 7 8 9 10 11	25 1 (2) 3 4 5	4
5	25	19	16	10	5 30	24	13	7	2 27	21	9 10 11 12 13 14	3 4 (5) 6 7 8	5
6	1 26	20	17	11	6 31	25	14	8	3 28	22	12 13 14 15 16 17	6 7 (8) 9 10 11	6
7	2 27	21	18	12	7	1 26	15	9	4 29	23	15 16 17 18 19 20	9 10 (11) 12 13 14	7
8	3 28	22	19	13	8	2 27	16	10	5 30	24	18 19 20 21 22 13	12 13 (14) 15 16 17	8
9	4 29	23	20	14	9	3 28	17	11	6 31	25	21 22 23 24 25 1	15 16 (17) 18 19 20	9
10	5 30	24	21	15	10	4 29	18	12	7	1 26	24 25 1 2 3 4	18 19 (20) 21 22 23	10
11	6 31	25	22	16	11	5 30	19	13	8	2 27	2 3 4 5 6 7	21 22 (23) 24 25 1	11
12	7	1 26	23	17	12	6	20	14	9	3 28	5 6 7 8 9 10	24 25 (1) 2 3 4	12

13	2 3 (4) 5 6 7	8 9 10 11 12 13	10 4 29	15	21	7	13	18	24	2 27	8	13
14	5 6 (7) 8 9 10	11 12 13 14 15 16	11 5 30	16	22	8	14	19	25	3 28	9	14
15	8 9 (10) 11 12 13	14 15 16 17 18 19	12 6	17	23	9	15	20	1 26	4 29	10	15
16	11 12 (13) 14 15 16	17 18 19 20 21 22	13 7	18	24	10	16	21	2 27	5 30	11	16
17	14 15 (16) 17 18 19	20 21 22 23 24 25	14 8	19	25	11	17	22	3 28	6 31	12	17
18	17 18 (19) 20 21 22	23 24 25 1 2 3	15 9	20	1 26	12	18	23	4 29	7	13	18
19	20 21 (22) 23 24 25	1 2 3 4 5 6	16 10	21	2 27	13	19	24	5 30	8	14	19
20	23 24 (25) 1 2 3	4 5 6 7 8 9	17 11	22	3 28	14	20	25	6 31	9	15	20
21	1 2 (3) 4 5 6	7 8 9 10 11 12	18 12	23	4 29	15	21	1 26	7	10	16	21
22	4 5 (6) 7 8 9	10 11 12 13 14 15	19 13	24	5 30	16	22	2 27	8	11	17	22
23	7 8 (9) 10 11 12	13 14 15 16 17 18	20 14	25	6 31	17	23	3 28	9	12	18	23
24	10 11 (12) 13 14 15	16 17 18 19 20 21	21 15	1 26	7	18	24	4 29	10	13	19	24
25	13 14 (15) 16 17 18	19 20 21 22 23 24	22 16	2 27	8	19	25	5 30	11	14	20	25

Note: Parenthesis ( ) means group begins a 120-hour leave at end of tour.

Figure 3-6
COMPARISON OF LEAVE NEEDED FOR THREE WEEKS VACATION UNDER THE TWO-PLATOON AND THREE-PLATOON CHARTS

		1	2	3	4	5	6	7	8
Three weeks leave:						(1	2	3	4
Days of the month:		1	2	3	4	5	6	7	8
Vacation days in the three-platoon, five-group chart schedule needed to get three weeks off	SCHEDULE	D	D	E	E		N	N	
		8	8	4	4	X	12	12	X
		8	4	12	12		8	8	
	VACATION						V	V	
	VACATION HOURS						8	8	
Vacation days in the two-platoon, twenty-five group chart schedule needed to get three weeks off	SCHEDULE	D	D	N	N				
		7	7	7	7	X	X	X	X
		7	7	7	7				
	VACATION								
	VACATION HOURS								
Days of the month:		1	2	3	4	5	6	7	8
Three weeks leave:						(1	2	3	4

X = Regular Day Off

D = Day 8A–4P or 8P
7A–7P

home later and waking up later the next day. Consequently, the time at home—not exactly quality hours to begin with—was further adversely affected.

By changing shifts at 7 a.m. and 7 p.m., the dispatcher saw most of his family awake for some part of every one of his fewer working days. After day tours he saw his wife and older kids,

5	6	7	8	9	10	11	12	13	14	15	16	17	18	19	20	21)					
9	10	11	12	13	14	15	16	17	18	19	20	21	22	23	24	25	26	27	28	29	30
		D	D	E	E		N	N				D	D	E	E		N	N			
X	X	8/4	8/8	4/12	4/12	X	12/8	12/8	X	X	X	8/8	8/4	4/12	4/12	X	12/8	12/8	X	X	X
		V	V	V	V		V	V				V	V	V	V						
		8	12	8	8		8	8				12	8	8	8	}	TOTAL HOURS 104				
D	D	N	N						D	D	N	N					D	D	N	N	
7/7	7/7	7/7	7/7	X	X	X	X	X	7/7	7/7	7/7	7/7	X	X	X	X	7/7	7/7	7/7	7/7	X
V	V	V	V						V	V	V	V									
12	12	12	12				12	12	12	12				}	TOTAL HOURS 96						
9	10	11	12	13	14	15	16	17	18	19	20	21	22	23	24	25	26	27	28	29	30
5	6	7	8	9	10	11	12	13	14	15	16	17	18	19	20	21)					

4P–12M   12M–8A
E = Evening   N = Night
7P–7A

since he generally was home by about 8 p.m. He could unwind at home during prime time or get to school and community events that were previously impossible for him to attend. He was far less likely to abuse alcohol opportunistically, since the situational excuse and opportunity were not the same as at midnight. Before his night tours, the dispatcher could spend time with his family since he generally did not leave for work until 6 p.m. Not only did the compressed working hours give the individual dispatcher more contingent time off, but it was structured in a way that provided him more opportunity for a more "normal" family life around his abnormal hours.

Reduced Number of Platoons. By reducing the number of platoons from three to two, the amount of managerial time spent on "housekeeping" chores is reduced while the operation continues to run smoothly. Management personnel have to contend with sick calls only twice daily instead of three times, and they are addressed at more "normal" hours. (Try calling around town at 11 p.m. to get somebody to come in for overtime—you wake up spouses and babies and usually make few friends!) This system allows managers more time for more consequential work such as planning and program design. It also gives you the opportunity to come in fresh in the morning since you're not up late at night resolving staffing problems.

Also, intershift communication times in the two-platoon system occur only twice a day. This leads to greater accuracy and consistency in the passing of administrative and operational messages ("What do you mean the night supervisor wasn't aware that the South Avenue drawbridge was stuck open? I told the day shift supervisor myself!").

Under this work chart there will be times when an individual dispatcher will work 48 hours within the normal seven-day work week, hence the consideration of costs associated with FLSA overtime regulations. There are many ways to deal with these occurrences. The eight hours of overtime worked on these occasions translate to 12 hours of comp time, which works out nicely with the 12-hour shifts. You can make any arrangement you want to deal with how these 12 hours are taken off. Generally the rules state that an employee who accumulates comp time must be permitted to use such time off within a reasonable period after making such request, if such time off would not unduly disrupt the operations of the agency. It is possible to calculate a fixed figure for the "scheduled overtime" in this work chart and simply include such payment on a once-a-year basis. It is also simplest just to pay the employee as the 48 hour week occurs. Nonetheless, this schedule offers so many benefits that it's worth the little extra effort involved in smoothing out the occasional wrinkle under the Wage and Hour Regulations.

Sample work charts are included for your examination. There are dozens of variations of these in use around the country. Changes in starting times, number of platoons, local labor laws, and different peak demand times are what usually dictate the differences. Now that you are aware of the far-reaching effects of work schedules, take a look at yours. Consider some of the physiological and social consequences of how your employees are scheduled to work. See if there is any room for a positive change in your operation.

CHAPTER FOUR

Personnel Management

YOUR DISPATCHERS SHOULD BE able to think quickly, use excellent judgment, and allocate resources correctly for the protection of the community. They must be able to give orders and direction to field forces under what are sometimes trying conditions. They should have strong, self-assured personalities. Paradoxically, the very qualities that we absolutely need to have in a first-class emergency communications dispatcher will sometimes give the ill-prepared manager the most difficulty in managing his personnel.

The dispatcher's strength and self-assurance springs in part from the knowledge that they do their jobs well. Confidence comes from competence. When it comes to taking orders, to having their working lives managed, they expect the same degree of competence from those who manage them. That expectation—desirable and predictable in a paramilitary organization that values and inculcates respect for rank and order—often conflicts with reality, given the circumstances under which promotions are made in most emergency service systems.

There are very few lateral entries into management positions in emergency communications. Almost all emergency communications managers are promoted from within the ranks of their departments. This is understandable. For one thing, the civil service systems in which many dispatchers operate do not usually allow for lateral entry. For another, emergency communications systems are usually so complex—requiring a thorough working knowledge of the department, its service capabilities, and its protection area—that it is hard to have somebody simply walk in and start managing the people who staff them. However, promoting from within often produces less than desired results. The system is flawed: Criteria on which promotions are made generally have little or nothing to do with managerial competence.

You may have an excellent attendance record. You may get along well with your fellow workers. You may know your job and do it well. You may be one of those people who are very good "test technicians" and score high on written exams. But none of these (or even all of these considered together) necessarily qualifies you to manage people. Many new managers promoted on the basis of such criteria soon discover that there are considerably more skills needed for a position that requires leadership, planning, organizing, and control (the four "classic" functions of management). Therefore, the expectation of managerial competency by competent workers quite frequently is one that goes unmet. The gap between this expectation and the reality of day-to-day functioning can be a source of friction and tension in your operation. How do you close this gap? Obviously, there are two ends from which to work toward the middle. On one hand, you can lower the expectation of competency. This runs counter to just about everything you want to do in your department. It deflates *esprit de corps.* It opposes the "can-do" attitude for which you strive in emergency services and fosters professional laziness. It is far more preferable for personnel to live up to expectations rather than live down to them. The second approach, *upgrading* your management of personnel, is far more desirable.

JOB ORIENTATION

The first step in making personnel management easier for both the manager and those being managed is to implement an effective employee orientation program. Too often, orientation is a haphazard experience for the new employee. Too often it is limited to cursory descriptions of physical and functional operational elements, such as "This is where we keep these forms" and "Here's how this transmitter works." Too often it makes a new employee perceive himself as being unable to fit in either technically or socially, which leads to attrition—after you've invested the time and money to attract and begin to train him. Often forgotten by management is why we conduct orientation in the first place. What do we want to achieve through the orientation process? What are the expected outcomes for both the employee and the department?

DEVELOPING A POSITIVE ATTITUDE

Orientation is the process by which new employees are introduced to the department, their tasks, their supervisors, their co-workers, and *to the department's philosophy of service.* The development of a positive attitude toward the department and toward the delivery of service starts here. Since "example is the best teacher," those who conduct the orientation should display a genuinely positive attitude toward the employees. Let the employee know that he is a valuable part of your operation. I can recall one dispatcher who, after he was photographed and fingerprinted, simply was given the name of a supervisor to whom he was to report. The dispatcher presented himself to his new boss at lunchtime, which didn't sit well with the personnel on duty: "You're the new guy? We thought you'd be here tomorrow. Aren't you supposed to stay with the personnel people for the first two days? Now what are we supposed to do? We only have enough food for six!" This new person was immediately made to feel like an outsider—as if he wasn't nervous enough on his first day on the job! Had there been some communication and preparation, he would not have been thrown into an unfamiliar situation and left to fend for himself.

Any established work group—in an office, on a construction gang, anywhere—is tough to break into. A working group of emergency communications dispatchers can be even more tightly knit. The hours, the pressures, and the social isolation that come with the territory can really promote a remarkable cohesiveness. When this unified group has shared goals with management, it can be a potent force for good service and easier management. When the group unification is of the "circle the wagons" variety in which an adversarial relationship between employees and management comes naturally, problems are generated. Productivity decreases, morale decreases, sick leave for both employees and managers increases, mistakes increase, labor relations costs (handling grievances, processing litigation, pursuing disciplinary actions) skyrocket. The sad part is that all of this is avoidable. You can preempt these developments with just a little care and concern. The way you introduce people to their work group is a detail that deserves your attention. The positive attitude, the sharing of department goals, and the productive emergency communications career all begin here.

DEVELOPING CLEARLY DEFINED WORK EXPECTATIONS

Make sure right now, during orientation, that your new employee knows exactly what is expected of him. Ideally, you should be reinforcing that which has already taken place in the evaluation and interview process. Hand the new employee a written job description. Use a written evaluation system that clearly defines tasks and standards of performance for those tasks.

A tandem evaluation form (see Figure 4-1, page 72)) will help to make sure that the employee comprehends all that's expected of him. Both the orientee and his instructor will have identical lists of items to be checked for minimal competency during the orientation; both will rate degrees of capability or knowledge as "Excellent," "Good," "Unsure," or "Needs Improvement." Any difference in their ratings on a specific item can be explored at the end of the day. In this way there is both validation of the instructor's perception of the orientee's skills and a nonthreatening means for the orientee to get clarification on any item that is unclear to him. For instance, if on the item "Is familiar with facility's fire safety procedures" the instructor rates the orientee as "Good" but the orientee checks "Unsure," there is an opportunity for two things to happen: First, the area of doubt in the orientee's mind can be addressed and resolved. Second, the instructor may find that, because the orientee demonstrated a working knowledge of the facility's handheld fire extinguishers, that didn't necessarily mean he was familiar with the halon fire suppression system in the computer room.

REDUCING EMPLOYEE ANXIETY

Note above that the tandem checklist provided was a *nonthreatening* means for the orientee to obtain clarification of task performance. Although no new employee anywhere wants to admit that he is nervous, it is especially uncomfortable to do so in the field of emergency communications. In this line of work the popular image is that you don't allow yourself to get flustered in any way. A new employee, totally unfamiliar with the system, may walk into a situation in which others working around him are apparently functioning smoothly, with no effort. This can be threatening. The employee may find himself thinking, I'll never be able to do this. How can they know what they're doing? How

Figure 4-1
ORIENTATION CHECKLIST

	Excellent	Good	Unsure	Needs Improvement
Understands work schedule				
Familiar with physical plant				
Knows location of fire extinguishers				
Processes box alarm				
Processes telephone alarm				
Understands leave request procedure				
Understands multiple-alarm notification procedure				

can they understand all those numbers so quickly? But he will not admit to any of those feelings *unless he is allowed to do so.* If the instructor explains to the orientee that it is normal to feel overwhelmed in the beginning, that everybody—including himself and the guys out there now barking numbers into radios and telephones—has felt "at sea" when he first walked in the door, then the new dispatcher will feel better about his likelihood of success in his new job.

Although it occurs in some form in just about every work setting, "hazing" of new employees is especially prevalent in emergency services. I remember dispatchers jumping up to salute delivery men whom they were told were off-duty chiefs. More than once a new dispatcher was instructed to call a company officer and ask if his company carried "fog chains" or a "Z-tool," or to park his car unknowingly in the chief's spot. While I don't recommend outlawing these "initiation rites" (unless, of course, they are mean-spirited; most are simply the products of active minds indulging in some fun in a place that is frequently exposed to tragedy), I would warn the orientee that such things generally occur. This allows him to expect these events *and* to be accepted by the other employees as well.

MAKING LIFE EASIER FOR SUPERVISORS AND CO-WORKERS

When I was a fire alarm dispatcher working on Brooklyn's newly installed computer-assisted dispatch system, I can recall a very difficult situation when a dispatcher was "detailed" from one of the other four boroughs. Since the department was still operating manual dispatch systems in Queens, Manhattan, Staten Island, and the Bronx, these detailed dispatchers were of little help in Brooklyn, except possibly as a radio operator (even then, they had to be familiar with Brooklyn's 129 units and hundreds of miles of streets). Every time one of the detailed members took a phone call he had to ask one of the Brooklyn dispatchers for assistance with getting the alarm into the computer system. It got so bad that several Brooklyn dispatchers filed grievances, saying that they were on duty for the purposes of providing fire protection, not computer training.

In any job, new employees will turn to supervisors and co-workers for help. If the employee had an effective orientation, more of this "breaking-in" will have already taken place, making life easier for others. Obviously, it is also more cost-effective to have employees performing their primary functions rather than out-of-title work. Sometimes there are less obvious costs associated with these kinds of events. In the Brooklyn grievance noted previously, I was one of the grievants. The whole process introduced me to the labor relations aspect of FDNY and to the union of which I eventually became president. Had the detailed dispatchers been properly trained, it is likely that I would not have bothered to pursue any interest in labor relations—an interest which ultimately cost FDNY a great deal of time and money.

SOCIAL ORIENTATION

In addition to functional and philosophical orientation, you can derive some benefit from a so-called "social orientation" that encourages employees to get to know their supervisors. It stresses that the employees should not be reluctant to initiate communication with their supervisors. Supervisors are presented in more personal terms, which enables the employee to view the supervisor as more than just "the boss." Furthermore, social orientation provides orientees with positive reinforcement as to their likelihood for success in their jobs. Experiments in which groups who received social orientation were compared with those who had not indicated that socially oriented employees exhibit less lateness, absenteeism, and wastefulness and require significantly less training time than their counterparts.

DEPARTMENT STRUCTURE

Management of personnel is further facilitated by having and using a clearly defined departmental structure. A Table of Organization should illustrate the relationship between the communications division and the rest of the department, the ranks of the division members, and the lines of responsibility, authority, and internal communication. It should also indicate the ratio of supervisors to employees at every level. Even if yours is a fairly small operation with only two dispatchers on duty at any given time, place one of those dispatchers in charge. Do this even if both personnel on duty have the same rank. You may find acceptance of this designation and its responsibility somewhat easier if you pay some sort of a differential for it, but do it in any case. By the same token, in the largest operations, where dozens of divisional dispatchers are on duty at any given time and there are middle layers of management personnel separating the working dispatcher from the person at the top, there still must be only one person in charge.

The principle of "unity of command" is very important in public safety service. There are several reasons for this, the most obvious encompassed by such sayings as "All chiefs and no Indians," "Too many cooks spoil the broth," and "No man can serve two masters." For the dispatcher, though, chain of command often seems to be in place just so that everything can slide down it and land on him! It appears so because the times when the chain of command is most diligently followed are the times when something is out of the ordinary or has been done wrong. The chain of command provides guidelines to follow in the event of a major disaster or other occurrence that requires upper-level command decisions. It also comes into use as an "audit trail"— the steps that supervisors retrace when following up on a complaint or a mistake of some sort. Actually, the audit trail provided by a firmly structured chain of command most often proves—as does the tape recorder which documents all phone calls and radio transmissions—that the dispatchers have done their jobs well.

Although we don't like to dwell on it because of our positive regard for public safety service, there are times when those in command simply are not performing their function correctly. The supervisor who is a substance abuser, for example, is not an unfamiliar story for many dispatchers. The folks who work directly under this supervisor need to know their recourse in such an event. A clearly defined Table of Organization can show a dispatcher the way to go with his problems. Also, when it's well-known that dispatcher orientees are made aware of their options should a supervisor behave irresponsibly, your supervisors will be less likely to behave in ways that will prompt their workers to seek such a resort. In this way the Table of Organization becomes part of the tightly knit management structure, as each part cross-supports another.

SUPPORT PERSONNEL

Although different operations have different needs, every emergency communications system requires a certain number of support personnel. I'm not talking about payroll people or employee benefits managers. These folks generally provide the same services for all the town, city, or county employees. By communications support personnel I mean linemen and cablemen (sometimes referred to as communications specialists); electricians; alarm assignment personnel; computer programmers; computer technicians; training officers; field communications/mobile command post personnel; engineers (for equipment design and procurement, radio repair and maintenance, outside plant installations—manholes, ductwork, working with the telephone company, etc.); planning and development personnel; and management information systems personnel.

FORMING A PARTNERSHIP

In smaller operations, support personnel for your emergency communications system frequently are shared with other public agencies. For instance, linemen who install and maintain the area's electricity delivery system may also be utilized in that capacity for alarm box circuitry. Similarly, computer technicians may be shared with the city's payroll and billing departments; engineers with the utilities departments; and planning and development personnel with the area's centralized planning office. In rural areas where often there is not enough tax revenue to support so many functions even when shared with other local agencies, regional planning commissions can provide the combined clout needed. State associations of various sorts often have the professional contacts that can help the emergency communications department meet its needs through contracted or consulting services. In all of these cases, "pooled" personnel perform what is essentially the same type of function for a variety of public agencies. Another option is for both department and nondepartment personnel to share the function.

But regardless of the way you get support personnel, some areas of your operation are going to require people who are trained in a discipline that's not traditionally associated with public safety service. You will be faced with the problem of blending their skills with your needs. The way to bridge this gap is by forming a partnership. For example, professionals who construct management information systems—the means by which you monitor productivity, assure quality, and systematically identify areas of strength and weakness—need considerable input from the communications managers who are going to be using the information. Then your people will need to be trained in how to use the generated data. Close cooperation between the folks who need the data and the people who set up the means to monitor, retrieve, and analyze it is essential.

Such cooperation is enhanced if your goals are clear to both sets of workers at the outset. Asking and answering some very basic questions will help to define these goals. What kind of data do I want? Why do I want it? In what way do I wish to measure it? Above all, to make your life as a manager of emergency communications personnel easier, make it absolutely clear who is in charge. Support personnel should support, not dictate. You should have the final say on any dispute between support personnel and communications personnel. Take advice and counsel from the experts, but make it clear that there *is* a hierarchy implied in the name *support* personnel.

"Turf wars" between the people in operations and the folks in support are manageable, with a little foresight. You should want people working for you who believe so strongly in what they do that they will fight for it. Whenever one of these skirmishes develops in a meeting, the emergency communications manager should not tiptoe around it. Note what is happening, make sure that the exchange does not degenerate into personal attack, and make it clear that you will have the final say.

Commenting on a conflict while it is happening—making note of the process as well as the content of what is going on in a meeting—often serves to defuse a situation. For example, your engineer wants a very loud alerting device attached to the alarm circuit from the local hospital. He reasons that, because of the life hazard involved, any alarm from this source should be heard above the ambient noise of the communications center. Your supervising dispatcher takes offense, feeling that the engineer thinks he and his dispatchers aren't good enough to distinguish the seriousness of such an alarm on their own, that they'll need some heavy electronic prompting. Rather than get into the middle of this battle, you should step back and invite the other participants to step back with you. "This is really gratifying to watch," you say. "I doubt that the people in this city realize that they have guys like you looking out for them with so much energy. Both of you guys are showing a lot of pride in your work and a lot of interest in protecting the people. I'm sure that nothing personal is meant here at all and I really appreciate your efforts. I've heard what both of you have said and I'll make a decision on it by the end of the day. Thanks for your intensity. Without it, we go stale!" The situation is depersonalized, all the participants are commended, and it is clear that you are in charge.

You'll note that several times now I've stressed the importance of making it clear to all involved who's the boss. This isn't because I expect all emergency communications managers to have problems with ego strength. It's just that a clear leader with a clear channel of accessibility—not just a line of command as delineated in your Table of Organization—is extremely important in any organization. I will add one more point of emphasis on this topic: Make sure that everybody knows who is in charge *at all times*. Emergency communications is a 24-hour endeavor. The worst personnel situations I've witnessed have developed during the "nonbusiness" hours and have usually been between operations and support people. In one case when a dispatch computer went down during a particularly busy alarm period, I saw angry dispatchers yelling at a poor programmer who had absolutely nothing to do with the computer's operation. The dispatchers were angry; the programmer was frustrated. The programmer worked long hours, as many programmers do. He was at the communications center late into the evening—an unsupervised support person. The dispatchers, who knew how to operate the CAD system but nothing else about it, figured that the "computer guy" should be responsible for whatever happened with the computer. The programmer had no one to turn to for direction. He felt, rightly, that he was under unjust attack and that he was on his own. For him, the best defense was a good offense, and he escalated the situation considerably. Only the intervention of cooler heads prevented a fistfight from developing. Now in that department there is a clearly designated person to whom dispatchers can turn when the system crashes. That person is a *dispatcher* who is assigned to computer operations and reports to the chief in charge. Because someone is clearly in charge, is an operations person, and has access to the leader, scenes like the one described above are not allowed to grow out of control.

Computerization of alarm assignments is another area in which problems have developed when support personnel are left to their own designs. Frequently the method in which computer personnel figure out unit response to a given location is to assign grid coordinates to both alarm box locations and firehouses. Addresses are usually already keyed to alarm box locations. It is then mathematically calculated who will be the closest to each possible alarm location according to the grid. If this process is left to the computer programmers, it will produce a workable system—for most cases. In emergency communications, you want a system which has an excellent chance of working in *all* cases! A flexible, farsighted communications department will allow seasoned dispatchers to work closely with the alarm assignment programmers and will benefit from that interaction. In large downtown areas, the closest units to a particular location may only be able to arrive first during certain hours of the day because of traffic patterns. Sometimes it's the apparent second-due units that have a far better shot at getting to a location fastest. A computer technician will not have the familiarity with traffic flow that a dispatcher has and cannot be expected to make allowances for it without assistance.

Services supplied by other support personnel are needed on a less regular basis than those supplied by computer people. Sharing these needs with a variety of other organizations and departments is an efficient, cost-saving way to meet the demand. If you plan to have your dispatchers CPR-certified, you may be able to secure the services of the local hospital's in-service educator. Local utilities may provide your dispatchers with some background on terminology and burn characteristics for specific transformers, manholes, and utility-pole hardware. Also, vendors are usually happy to provide training in the use of their products and it's often written into service contracts.

If you are fortunate enough to have a specified training officer, he should have a clearly delineated line of authority in your department's Table of Organization. Once again, your department's structure should make management easier. If you do not have a training officer, your efforts to secure other means of training will go a long way toward making the dispatcher feel that you are investing in him. You are making his work more stimulating and challenging him to grow professionally. This, too, should make your management of personnel a far easier job.

PERFORMANCE EVALUATION
OF SUPPORT PERSONNEL

Evaluating support personnel can present a challenge for the emergency communications manager. If you are a former dispatcher (as most emergency communications managers are), it is easy for you to assess the work of your dispatchers. But how do you evaluate the performance of professional engineers? Of computer techs?

The answer lies in taking the time to have a very structured and well-documented working relationship with support personnel. Even though these folks may be working for the city or county, just as you are, deal with them as you would with contractors.

Planning. Have regular planning sessions with your support personnel. Have an agenda to which all parties can contribute. Keep minutes that all parties can approve and refer to in the future.

Measurable expected outcomes. You need not have gone to engineering school to know how you want something to come out. You do need to know if your expectations are reasonable. Is what you are asking physically doable? Is it financially possible? Mutual agreement on expected outcomes and performance measurements is essential.

Do you want to be sure that your CRTs don't crash if the local power supply is interrupted? Do you want the same headset to interface with both the radio and telephone systems? Do you want to have a remote starter button for your emergency generator? Do you want your computer to display a map that can show unit locations? Address locations? In plain, straightforward language, explain what you would like to have happen. Ask your engineer, programmer, or technician if it is possible to have this capacity in your system. If the answer is no, ask for reasons; if the answer is yes, request an outline of costs and an expected completion date.

Accountability. Suppose that the answer is no, the reasons why are listed, and you don't understand the first damned thing the engineer said in his report! Usually if the message in an engineer's or a programmer's report is that obscure, it's because he wanted to make it that way. He may feel that if he utilizes your suggestion people may ask why he didn't think of it in the first place. Maybe he's just plain lazy. Or maybe he just isn't aware that there is a way to do what you want to do. In any case, what can you do when he says it can't be done and you've seen it work perfectly in the next county?

You will find that many of your ideas for equipment modifications and installations do indeed come from your visits to other communications centers. You see something you like and imagine how much easier it would make work for your dispatchers back home. If you run into a roadblock in getting the idea implemented, call the place where you saw it working. Ask who their vendor is and give him a call. Equipment manufacturers can provide a lot of help in explaining how their goods can satisfy your needs. Meet with the manufacturer's representative and share the objections raised by your support people. If there's a way to get done what you want done, the rep will find it. After all, he wants to make the sale.

When you do this a few times, the message will be clear that you expect your support people to look into things carefully. After a while if a report comes back that a certain piece of equipment is not compatible with your system, the report will note that the engineer or the computer tech (or whoever) has indeed met with the manufacturer's rep, and that the rep concurs with the conclusion. The support person's accountability for substantiating his position will become a given.

Make sure that all of your interactions in measuring the performance of your support personnel are well documented (see Figure 4-2 on page 84). The purpose of the documentation is not to build a case against somebody. It is primarily for communication purposes. Share the documentation with those involved so there can be little room for misinterpretation. Documentation, of course, also provides you with the audit trail which is necessary for effective and orderly management. Ultimately, all of this effort translates to a more efficient emergency communications system.

EVALUATION OF DISPATCH PERSONNEL

The nature of the emergency communications business is such that individual operational mistakes are usually apparent immediately. When there is an acute time value attached to the work you do, it does not take long for somebody to spot an error. I remember an alarm for a vacant building fire at 4 a.m. in which the normal alarm assignment called for a battalion chief from one firehouse and the fire companies from two other firehouses. When the chief rolled up to the building all by his lonesome, it became apparent rather quickly that something had gone wrong. He knew that no other fire activity had tied up the other four units, since he would have been with them. If one of his first-alarm units had been relocated to cover a temporarily stripped neighborhood, he would have been notified by the radio dispatcher that he was going in with an altered assignment. Had there been an apparatus accident, he most likely would have heard about it on the radio, but that would have meant four separate accidents (or two accidents, each of which involved two units!). Consequently, the chief knew that there had been an error made somewhere along the line. The chief gave notice of solitary arrival, upon which the dispatcher checked his voice alarm panel (the console through which verbal messages were sent to firehouses) and noted that a necessary zone button had not been pushed. The chief's zone received the message, but the button for verbal transmission of the alarm to the firehouses in the first-alarm zone was not activated.

Figure 4-2
DOCUMENTATION OF SUPPORT STAFF PERFORMANCE

TO: Ralph Flots, County Computer Programmer

FROM: Joe Smith, Chief of Fire Communications

DATE: 8/1/90

SUBJECT: Duplicate Street Names

Dear Ralph,

As we discussed yesterday, a problem encountered with our new CAD system is that several towns in our county have "Main" streets. It is my understanding that by Sept. 1, 1990 you will have in place a program which will suggest several town options to our county fire dispatchers if they enter "Main Street" as an alarm location.

kth

cc: county commissioner
    fire chiefs
    managers

Document all interactions with support personnel so that communication is unified. The "cc" list keeps all those involved on the same channel.

Not only was it immediately apparent that there was a problem, but the system was such that it could be determined who had made the mistake. Furthermore, it could be ascertained that the error had two components: the manual mistake of not pressing all the right buttons and the operational gaff of not receiving a verbal acknowledgement of the alarm from the units assigned to the fire. The dispatcher at the voice alarm console could more easily have been excused for the manual error than for the sheer sloppiness of not listening for message acknowledgment from the units. The regulation requiring a verbal acknowledgement to a run was the systemic check designed to balance such errors as not pressing all the right buttons. By failing to observe that regulation, the dispatcher compounded what had been a fairly innocuous error. It was now both serious (in terms of the advanced stage of fire development that would greet the delayed units on their arrival) and public (by virtue of the chief's message, "Where are my companies?" heard on scanners throughout the city and recorded on tape at headquarters).

You can see, then, that because of the urgent nature of the work and the layers of redundancy that are usually built into emergency communications operations, *identifying* the mistakes is not usually the problem. *Reacting* to them is the challenge.

Discipline. The less room there is for "free-lancing" in reaction to problems, the better. A primary means of avoiding the inconsistency that comes with "ad-lib discipline" is to establish clearly defined rules and well-delineated consequences for breaking them. These are usually covered during orientation. However, some managers, concerned about appearing too negative at this point in the employee's fledgling relationship with the department, gloss over the rules, make some small passing reference to them, or completely ignore them altogether. Despite the concern, it is necessary to inform employees of the regulations. While the "job expectations" part of orientation covers the tasks and standards specific to a job, there are other more general rules of which the employee must be made aware. The easiest way to do this is to hand him the rules and make it known that he's expected to respect them.

Beyond the performance expectations for the dispatcher's job, every employee of your municipality is covered by rules pertaining to such items as general conduct, sick leave, lateness, jury duty, drug and alcohol use, and so forth. Grounds for disciplinary action should be clearly defined (see Figure 4-3). If you are dealing with unionized workers, their contract with you will clearly spell out discipline, appeal, and grievance procedures.

As a guideline, "three strikes and you're out" is a fairly reliable philosophy. Depending, of course, on the severity and frequency of the offense, the course of disciplinary action usually runs from a verbal warning to a written warning to suspension from duty. Both verbal and written warnings need to be documented, with a written acknowledgment from the employee. Some managers might object, saying that documentation of a verbal warning makes it a written warning. Not so. You give the verbal warning: "Ralph, this is the fourth time you've been late this month. I'm sure there are reasons in each case, but I'm equally sure that you want to get relieved on time just as much as the guys you are relieving. You know that we're a 24-hour operation here and that nobody can walk away from their post until relieved. We have to work together and serve the people. Consequently, I'm asking you to give some more attention to being on time. If there is another incidence of lateness in the next ninety days, you'll get a written warning." You then document this with a memo, which is signed by the employee. He gets a copy, his file gets a time-limited copy (that is, the date on which it will be expunged from his file is clearly stated in the memo—in the case of a first warning, usually ninety days), and you keep a copy in your file of "anecdotal" personnel records (informal notes to yourself regarding employee performance that list dates, times, places, people, and details involved in any action you have to take as a manager whereby possible personnel action—discipline, commendation, award—may result). (See Figure 4-4.) This is not a written warning. It is documentation of a verbal warning. It is necessary to show that you are doing your job, to show that less severe steps were taken if the time comes for a written warning, and to provide managerial continuity should you retire, be promoted, or take any kind of leave.

Suspension is followed by a hearing (in some jurisdictions,

Figure 4-3
OUTLINING GROUNDS FOR DISCIPLINARY ACTION

FIRE DEPARTMENT

DISCIPLINARY GUIDELINES

These disciplinary guidelines are provided for your information and do not constitute a contract. It is hoped that you will not have cause to refer to these guidelines during the course of your career, either as the employee being charged or the employee preferring charges.

Offenses are divided into three categories, according to their severity. While some offenses are naturally considered to be more serious than others, none of these offenses is considered minor. The following list is a synopsis. For more complete details, you are referred to the Department's Personnel Manual.

These guidelines are to be posted in all Department work sites.

Category I: Violations in this category will result in a reprimand being entered in your personnel record. Where appropriate, restitution may be required. The offenses included discourtesy, selling of raffle tickets without Department permission, offensive language, gambling on Department premises, loss or damage of Department property, excessive lateness.

Category II: Violations in this category will result in a disciplinary hearing. Possible outcomes include fines, forfeiture of annual leave time, and/or termination of employment. The offenses include repeated violations in Category I, AWOL, fighting on Department property, making a false statement with intent to deceive, feigning illness, disrespect of a superior, selling or giving away Department property.

Category III: Violations in this category will result in immediate suspension from duty. A disiciplinary hearing will be scheduled. The offenses include repeated violations of Category II, felony conviction, disobeying a direct order, being under the influence of alcohol and/or drugs while on duty.

Figure 4-4
ANECDOTAL PERSONAL RECORD

Employee: Joe Smith

Date	Action Taken
7/4/89	Commendation for Duty Under Trying Circumstances
11/29/89	Unit citation from mayor to all dispatchers for duty in recent brushfire season
5/6/90	Verbal warning: 35 minutes late for day shift. Expectation: No lateness for 90 days or loss of shift exchange privilege will result.
9/12/90	No lateness past 90 days

it's called a "departmental trial") to determine one of three possible outcomes: (1) no grounds for discipline, restore to duty without prejudice; (2) penalty imposed—this could be a fine, loss of accrued leave time, transfer, or (in a civil service system) reduction in grade; or (3) separation from service. The hearing can be held before a chief, the board of county commissioners, the city personnel director, or whomever your department designates. Just be sure that if you come to a decision to terminate an employee, an attorney is consulted before the decision is released. If a contested decision goes to litigation, remember that you are expected to be a manager, not a lawyer. You are expected to reduce risks and liabilities but not to make legal judgments.

Having a place on your disciplinary forms for an attorney to sign when the termination stage is reached is a built-in check against unnecessary risk (see Figure 4-5).

All supervisory personnel must be aware of the need for consistency in disciplinary matters. While some obvious infractions such as drinking on duty are not subject to much second-guessing when it comes to discipline, others such as "conduct tending to bring reproach or reflect discredit upon the department" are open to a great deal of subjective interpretation. This

Figure 4-5
DISCIPLINARY FORM SIGN-OFFS

Accordingly, it has been determined that Dispatcher Walsh has shown such repeated disregard for the Rules and Regulations of the Department that his employment is terminated as of close of business this date.

_____

Ralph Kramer, Chief Dispatcher

_____

Jim Benson, Fire Commissioner

_____

Steve Foss, Esq., Counsel to Blue Hills County

translates to a high potential for abuse. The last thing a manager wants to hear as a defense is the allegation from an employee that some other supervisor "allows his guys to do it, so what's the big deal?" The principal reason why you don't want to hear this is because it's usually accurate! But even worse is the defendant's allegation that the supervisor himself "does it"—"Sure I had alcohol on my breath. Ralph (the supervisor) bought the wine we had with dinner!" In addition to consistency in matters of discipline, supervisors must also be aware of the fact that you expect role modeling from them and that you will not tolerate anything less than the best on-duty behavior from them.

Above all, keep discipline on a "strictly business" plane. No emotionalism. No personal attacks. No like response to the personal attacks of others. Simple, efficient documentation, with employee's written acknowledgment where appropriate, leads to easier execution of what can be—if it is allowed to be—one of the hardest parts of the manager's job.

Praise. Besides dealing with problems, the evaluation process should be geared for more than equal time devoted to identifying strengths and giving encouragement for good work. Let's face it: Although it sometimes *seems* that you spend most of your managerial time dealing with mistakes and shortcomings, the reason why such incidents stand out is that they are *unusual.* What is usual is that your emergency communications center hums along, providing reliable service. Never take this routine level of efficiency for granted. Sure, "that's what they're paid to do"; what *you're* paid to do is see that they keep operating at this desirable plateau. Praise, both informal and structured, goes a long way toward letting the dispatcher know that his work is noted and appreciated.

Regarding informal managerial comments on performance, ask yourself, How often do I let my people know that I like what they are doing? How often do I complain? Just as a preponderance of complaints ultimately has a negative effect on morale and performance, routine positive reinforcement can deliver a cumulative dividend of generally happier and more productive employees. Now I hear several of you at this point asking, "*Happier* employees? He wants us to worry about employees' *happiness*? He thinks we have time for this?" The answer to the above questions is "Yes!" Consider what happens when you have unhappy employees: mistakes, increased sick leave, grumbling, nobody going the extra mile to deliver service, lateness. All of which will demand your time and attention as a manager. So, yes, you will have the time—you'll want to *make* the time—to worry about the happiness of your dispatchers. If you have not been attending to the positive aspects of your people's performance, you may have to make the time at first. But it is worth the investment.

Dispatchers have been characterized as the "forgotten professionals" of emergency services. Because they are professionals, they can usually understand why that is so when it comes to a general public they anonymously protect. They are less tolerant of being forgotten by the people who know and understand the job they do, the people who, unlike the general public, see the dispatchers every day: their bosses.

Beyond the necessary day-to-day praise, more notable kinds of performance require more formal recognition. There are several ways to do this.

Individual Commendation. This frequently comes in the form of a letter from the chief in charge of the communications operation (division, bureau, section, or whatever). Outstanding acts are most often recognized, usually through a letter of praise from a civilian or from a local official. Of course, these should be emphasized by the manager, but it's also important to be sensitive to the acts of your dispatchers that might be unrelated to emergency duty yet prominent nonetheless. One dispatcher who, during a ferocious snowstorm, put on her cross-country skis and skiied some seven miles to her post at the county emergency operations center comes to mind immediately. By the same token, you should not limit your letters of commendation to notice of conspicuous acts. A dispatcher who has a year's perfect attendance is worthy of note, as is the person who regularly volunteers for needed extra duties. (Figure 4-6.)

Although the personal letter has the most positive impact, there is also the option of issuing a certificate of commendation or a plaque to the individual. Although they're less personal than the letter, some folks like to frame them and hang them on their basement walls. They do give someone the opportunity to be publicly proud of his work.

Group Commendation. Depending on the size of your operation, this can be awarded to the entire dispatching force or to a particular group of dispatchers who performed well during a demanding period. While usually you will be the one to present the award, encourage others to become involved. Commendations can be initiated by a line supervisor or suggested by a member of the field forces, too. Make sure that your line supervisors are aware of the value that your department places on praise of good work: include space on their evaluation forms

Figure 4-6
LETTER OF COMMENDATION

Presented to Dispatcher Joe Smith upon the occasion of his chairmanship of the Christmas Toy Drive for the East Arnold Fire Department. His continuing selfless efforts have brought cheer to hundreds of area children and have reflected positively on our department and its members.

Ralph Kramer
Fire Chief

whereby they can clearly note whether or not they commend employees under their supervision.

Suggestion Awards. The people who are doing the job every day are most often the people who are going to have the best ideas on how to improve it. Since they are in line positions, they are not involved in the organization at a policy-making level. You can tap this fruitful source of ideas, though, by establishing a "suggestion awards" program. A form that contains the criteria for submitting entries (see Figure 4-7 on page 94) can be posted at a bulletin board, time clock, or wherever personnel are most likely to see and use it. The form should also list the process by which the suggestions are reviewed and the awards given. Designate a review committee or make suggestion review a function of an active committee. Decide how often you will judge the ideas submitted and what you will offer for the winners. Usually, a nominal amount of cash is given to the periodic winners, with a more substantial prize for an annual "top suggestion." In some cases, days off are awarded. In any case, be sure and acknowledge all suggestions. Regardless of whether you can actually use them or not, they represent an employee's time and effort devoted to improving the operation.

Public Relations. Anytime you have cause to commend an employee, you have a positive public relations opportunity. The form that this PR takes depends on what the commendation is for. If you are recognizing one year of perfect attendance, a mention in the department's newsletter is appropriate. If you are commending ten years of no absences, a press release to local papers, complete with a photo of the chief presenting the citation to the commended employee, is in order.

Similarly, winners of suggestion awards can be highlighted in local and in-house media. Besides letting all of the employee's friends and relatives see that he is doing well at work, such exposure also gives the citizens who support the service the message that they have some quality folks working for them.

Some departments hold an annual affair where they recognize

Figure 4-7

COMMUNICATIONS DIVISION
SUGGESTION FORM

Name:

Date:

Please describe the situation that you would like to improve.

Please describe your SUGGESTION for this improvement. Be sure to include how your idea will improve operations, increase morale or productivity, or decrease costs.

Use the other side of this form or attach additional sheets if necessary.

Thank you for your suggestion. Your interest in improving our operation helps make us the best at what we do. Your suggestion will be reviewed at the next monthly meeting of the chief and commissioners. You will be notified in writing of their response. Savings bonds are awarded quarterly to members whose suggestions are implemented. The best suggestion of the year is officially recognized at the Department's annual dinner.

excellence with structured awards for meeting certain criteria. These can be for heroism, administrative excellence, attendance, productive suggestions, or community service. Because community service most often involves a member's activities outside of the department, departments often underestimate its usefulness in creating a positive public image, in aiding recruitment, and in increasing departmental pride. You should be aware of the benefits to the department when official recognition is given to off-duty activities such as Big Brothers/Big Sisters, Meals on Wheels, Boy Scouts, and the like. There is a lot of positive splashover for the department in the community. By highlighting these kinds of activities among its members, a department may attract the potential employee who sees the story in his local paper or on the six o'clock news and thinks he might like to work with a group of people like that. And the honored employee knows that the department views him as more than just a cog in the gears—it is recognizing him as a person as well as a dispatcher.

RAISES

Obviously, one of the principal ways of recognizing excellence is to "put your money where your mouth is." While all of the aforementioned techniques for praising your employees are valuable and effective, they start to ring a little hollow if you don't back them up with some bucks. I have been at award ceremonies during which I heard dispatchers' wives comment, "The plaque is very nice, but it doesn't pay the rent." Because of the nature of dispatchers' low-visibility work, it is often hard to sell authorities on its value. Taxpayers always have a hard time funding any "just-in-case" services. When they do, it is easiest for them to understand the high-visibility components. When there is an auto accident, the picture in the paper shows the rescue truck. Firefighters silhouetted against a burning building at night make an impressive image. When do the taxpayers ever see dispatchers?

In some jurisdictions where dispatchers are also building receptionists and *are* on display, the dispatchers create their own worst images by having piles of books and magazines sitting around their work stations, surrounded by empty styrofoam cups and half-eaten salami sandwiches. To the average citizen walking in the door looking for a brush-burning permit, it looks like these guys are getting paid to sit on their butts, read, and eat! We in the business all know that, indeed, there *are* times when all a dispatcher will do is sit and wait. However, he can certainly look good while he's doing it!

How you arrive at dispatchers' salaries depends on far many more factors specific to your location (service demands, population, tax base, and other resources) than can be dealt with here. But no matter where you start, how you give raises is a topic that bears exploration.

CIVIL SERVICE

If you find yourself in a well-established county or city civil service system, you most likely are dealing with an annual "across-the-board" style of awarding raises. All county employees get a percentage increase that's already been determined by a number of political factors that almost never have anything to do with performance. There are traditional pros and cons to this system. To my way of thinking, however, even the pros have cons. One of the most often cited positive aspects of this business method is the security afforded employees of this system. True, they are protected from "purges" every time the party in power changes, and from nepotism. However, they are also "protected" from the consequences of lousy work! "Job security" becomes "job stagnation." For people in emergency communications, lethargy simply should have no place at all.

How many times have you heard the phrase "civil service reform"? Most often in an election year, someone who is "out" and wants to be "in" decides that it is time to get rid of the "dead wood" in the civil service system. Invariably, "reform" comes to mean "terminate." The fact is, you will always have civil service and you will always have a certain number of employees in that system with the "civil service mentality." A real reformer might do well to look at positive prospects for change rather than just the negative, rather than adopting the heavy-handed, quick-fix approach. Besides dealing with the drawbacks inherent in a system that rewards inertia, the good manager in such a system experiences some frustration in being *unable to reward excellence*. In some cases, it is possible to make modifications to provide a semblance of a merit pay structure within a civil service system. An employee who rates an outstanding evaluation, for example, can be boosted a step or a grade, in addition to receiving simply what his co-workers in that jurisdiction get. The smaller your system, the easier this kind of "reform" is. Larger systems are that much more ponderous and it is difficult to effect any change in them within the length of the average career!

MERIT

We have been discussing employee evaluation in the terms in which most people think of it: discipline and praise. Yet the vast bulk of performance is consistently acceptable and usually lies between the extreme "goods" or "bads" that may cause the manager to think in terms of either praise or discipline. There is a system that responds to this reality, while also allowing for the extremes.

If you find yourself in a non-civil service situation, you may wish to consider a merit pay system. In such a system you must have an evaluation tool that is closely related to your job description and that allows for measurement of degrees of proficiency (see Figure 4-8). Your evaluation tool should be closely related to your job description. Breaking the job description down into specific areas to be rated allows the evaluator to address clearly both the positive and negative aspects of an employee's performance. Requiring an explanation for extreme ratings serves to keep the evaluator on his toes by reducing the possibility for favoritism or negative personal influence and gives the employee very specific feedback on his performance. Just as the rating tool is closely related to the job description, the specifics of an unsatisfactory rating should be included in a work improvement plan. You can use as many categories as you like and describe them in any fashion that suits you. Your best employees may be classified as "outstanding" or "excellent," your average employees as "acceptable," Your below-average workers as "marginal" or "unsatisfactory." Whatever terminology you choose, be sure and include with the evaluation tool a clear definition of the grades and what their consequences are (see Figure 4-9 on page 100). Make sure that the consequences for each rating are clearly spelled out in a sheet that is handed to each dispatcher at orientation and at the start of each rating period. Even though termination is an extreme outcome and unlikely, do not hesitate to cover that ground at the outset. That way a difficult employee is less likely to be able to claim surprise when any disciplinary action is initiated.

Depending on what your budget planners have determined as the average ("acceptable") allowable amount of increase available for that year, your "outstanding" and "excellent" employees would fall into a higher increase category, and your "marginal" and "unsatisfactory" employees would receive less than the average increase (or perhaps would receive no increase at all but rather would be placed on probation pending improvement of performance). The distribution would resemble a bell curve for the number of dispatchers in each percentage rating (see Figure 4-10). They would not necessarily fall into such an even distribution for absolute dollars, however, since many of your "outstanding" employees are also those who have been employed the longest. Consequently, they usually have a higher base before the raise is calculated; giving them any increase requires more dollars than giving a similarly rated increase to an employee with fewer years of service.

The group, as a whole, though, would receive the average percentage increase. A worksheet that helps to keep your evalua-

Figure 4-8
PERFORMANCE EVALUATION

DISPATCHER EVALUATION   Name:
Page Three

Competency   Rating (O, A, U)

XIV. Public Relations

This area of competency is evaluated by listening to
your work, either directly or on tape; and by considering
written commendations or complaints from members of
the public and the department.

Courtesy:

Accuracy of information given:

Referral approprlateness:

Dispatcher identified at
beginning of conversation:

Evaluator explanation for "Outstanding" or "Unac-
ceptable" ratings:

XV. Media Relations:

Courtesy:

Media Liason Officer Notified:

Figure 4-9
RATINGS AND CONSEQUENCES

EXPLANATION OF RATINGS

Outstanding—In order to be rated "Outstanding" in a particular competency, a dispatcher must consistently perform at a level clearly above that expected by the department to meet minimal competency. This work must be recognized by co-workers, supervisors, or members of the public we serve as being of outstanding caliber. "Outstanding" ratings must have supporting documentation from the evaluator. An "Outstanding" rating overall will result in the employee so rated receiving an annual pay increase two percent above the "Acceptable" rate for that year.

Acceptable—In order to be rated "Acceptable" in a particular competency, a dispatcher must consistently perform at a level which clearly demonstrates that he meets the department's performance expectations for his job description.

Unsatisfactory—A dispatcher who fails to meet the department's performance standards in a particular competency will be rated "Unsatisfactory" for that competency and will be given a 90-day period in which to improve that particular competency. A specific work improvement plan, with clearly outlined and measurable goals and objectives, will be provided to help the dispatcher make the desired improvement. An "Unsatisfactory" rating in three or more competencies will result in delay of any salary review until the end of the 90-day improvement period. An overall "Unsatisfactory" rating, or failure to improve in areas consistently rated "Unsatisfactory," will result in disciplinary review. Termination of employment is one possible outcome of such a review. For further information on disciplinary review, see your Personnel Handbook.

tions within budget range can easily be developed from existing salary information (see Figure 4-11). This sheet shows what your current personnel are making, what each percentage increase would mean in terms of dollars and cents per hour, and the dollar figure that is the ceiling under which you should try to keep the total of all the increases in the unit. The distribution in Figure 4-11 shows a unit with 10 employees and an anticipated average increase of five percent. The total of actual increases ($4.63) is slightly above five percent. However, three of the 10 employees are rated above average. The worksheet is designed to provide general guidelines to help the manager stay within budget.

You should not, however, be absolutely bound by such a sheet to give a dispatcher less than what is deserved. If you have

Figure 4-10
BELL CURVE FOR PERFORMANCE RATINGS

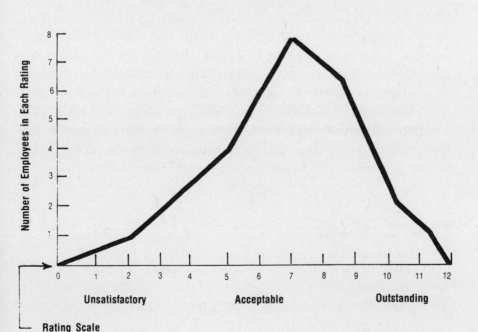

more than the expected number of personnel whose performance places them on the right-hand side of your unit's percentage increase curve, don't feel that you have to alter your evaluations to meet your finances. Count yourself lucky to have such quality personnel and try to find the money somewhere in your budget to pay them!

As noted, this system does respond to the extremes in performance. However, in any system it is likely that response to at least the negative extremes takes the form of disciplinary procedures. And, occasionally, stand-out work is at least acknowledged (if not always rewarded) in most systems. What the merit pay system adds to this is a continuing feedback to the average employee. The individual worker gets a sense that he is *not* "lost between the cracks" in the organization. And the supervisor continually examines the employee's performance according to the objective criteria outlined in the performance evaluation tool. There is a built-in quality assurance factor here.

When I worked in FDNY, the New York City Civil Service System was the overall source of personnel management resources. While there were both outstanding dispatchers and lousy dispatchers, and everybody from the chiefs to their co-workers knew who they were, the only financial reward anybody got was an across-the-board percentage increase. The outstanding worker received the same as the marginal worker—a true disincentive to productivity. The merit pay system will allow you to keep the unit of employees generally within the bounds of an agreed-upon percentage increase while avoiding the professional stagnation that an across-the-board system engenders.

PROMOTIONS

A promotion is another concrete example of employer reward for performance. It is different from other performance rewards in several ways. For one thing, many employees never experience

Figure 4-11
SALARY BUDGET WORKSHEET

PERSONNEL	HOURLY RATE	POSSIBLE INCREASES			NEW RATE	ACTUAL INCREASE
		3%	5%	7%		
ɔbinson	$10.57	.32 inc./hr. 10.89 ttl./hr.	.53 11.10	.74 11.31	11.31	.74
arroll	8.65	.26 8.91	.43 9.08	.61 9.26	9.08	.43
gram	8.65	.26 8.91	.43 9.08	.61 9.26	8.91	.26
ɔhnson	7.69	.23 7.92	.38 8.07	.54 8.23	8.23	.54
e	9.62	.29 9.91	.48 10.10	.67 10.29	10.10	.48
ɔlger	7.69	.23 7.92	.38 8.07	.54 8.23	8.07	.38
avis	7.69	.23 7.92	.38 8.07	.54 8.23	8.07	.38
ese	8.65	.26 8.91	.43 9.08	.61 9.26	9.08	.43
anley	8.65	.26 8.91	.43 9.08	.61 9.26	9.26	.61
ɔldberg	7.69	.23 7.92	.38 8.07	.54 8.23	8.07	.38
ɔTALS	$85.55	$2.57	$4.28	$5.99		$4.63

a promotion. For another, unlike a raise, in which the employee gets more money for doing the same work, a promotion is a move upward to a different position. There are usually different responsibilities, duties, and privileges involved. Selecting a candidate for promotion is in some ways similar to the selection of dispatcher candidates discussed in Chapter Two. Basically, you want to describe what the job entails (position description) and to pick the right person for the job, and you'll have established criteria to help you in this process. Of course, in the promotion process, you have the advantage of familiarity with the candidates. Rather than trying to predict blindly how a person will perform in a position, you have the aid of several years of performance evaluations.

The most frequently cited criteria for promotion are merit and seniority. Even outside of either civil service or unionized settings, seniority is a very strong influence on advancement decisions. The argument is that experience leads to expertise. Other arguments for seniority-based promotions are that they are impartial and reward loyalty to the department. On the other hand, experience does not *always* lead to expertise, and use of seniority as the only promotion standard allows plenty of room for those less talented with longevity to move to the top. This is quite discouraging for your sharp younger employees.

There are several other factors that usually come into play in most promotion decisions. Political pressure is not to be discounted in any system, whether it be from departmental or governmental sources. The fire service is most often a government-funded service. As such, it is necessarily subject to the same influences as any public operation. In civil service systems, where the idea is to avoid or minimize political influence in job matters, political pressures are often realized in "exempt" or "provisional" positions. In non-civil service systems, many a "councilman's cousin" shows up in the ranks of government employees. In neither case is the outcome necessarily bad. But you must be aware of the presence of that influence if you are to operate your system successfully. Sometimes, you will not be able to put people where you want them. The best you can do is to document this thoroughly in your correspondence, or at least in your anecdotal records. If the political appointee turns out to be as bad a performer as you had predicted, you want to be covered, not crucified!

Another influence in any promotion that's not rigidly governed by testing is the personality of the candidates. For folks in emergency communications, this is not at all a bad consideration. I took my first communications job at the age of eighteen, with absolutely no idea of what it entailed. All I knew was that it offered the salary and hours I wanted. When I asked the boss, who had been in emergency communications for decades, what the qualifications were, he said one thing: "You gotta have the disposition for it." In many ways, he was right. There is a certain intangible quality about a good dispatcher.

That "intangible" wouldn't cut any ice in the arena of the last concern we'll mention about promotions: a court of law. We have all seen newspaper stories in which courts have ordered promotions. This is sometimes done on the basis of historical bias—in a case, for instance, in which all supervisory personnel in a certain department over the last forty years have been Caucasians while the department consists of 25 percent minority employees, some who are eligible for a promotion; or in a case in which all managerial personnel making promotion decisions are men and there are no female supervisors. In cases such as these, you have to take an *honest* look at your department's practices. If you find that there is a basis for such an action, besides a healthy reaction to the intrinsic injustice involved you have a managerial responsibility to protect your department by notifying the appropriate authorities. Once again, when something does eventually come to the surface (and it will), you will be on record as having made the proper preventive efforts. Be aware that wherever incompetence is involved, the incompetent will be looking for a scapegoat. Protect yourself with paper.

In summary, promotions are influenced by merit, seniority, politics, personality of the candidate, and the law. Other than that, they're easy!

UNIONS

Whenever you are dealing with a union, the rules change drastically. If yours is an operation that has not yet become unionized and you hope to continue to avoid unionization, pay attention to your employees! Unions flourish in direct proportion to the ineptitude of management. If management was beneficent and wise enough to deal properly with its workers, then the employees wouldn't feel the need to pay somebody else to see that it was done correctly.

I was a municipal union president. For five years, I represented the 200 dispatchers and supervisors in the FDNY Bureau of Fire Communications. Even though we were a small unit by Big Apple standards (there were more than 200,000 city employees), I frequently was able to get at least 30 seconds of air time on local evening news broadcast and a lot of column inches of newsprint in the local papers. There were two reasons for this. One was the incredible sensitivity and importance of the job itself. It holds people's interest because they know that the dispatcher is their first line of defense in times of urgent need. The second reason was that the degree of incapability displayed by many of the city's managers was so staggering that it made great copy.

Spare yourself the embarrassment of having a local reporter ask if it's true that your people work six days a week and haven't had a vacation in 18 months. Avoid the upset stomach you'll get when you listen to the radio and hear that you refused comment when asked if it was true that your new fire alarm boxes weren't working as planned. Preempt the predicament that results when the local councilman shows up at the door with a video crew, wanting to see the toilets that don't work, the rats in the base-ment of the communications center, and the chained exit doors in fire headquarters. Do the right and responsible thing for your employees and you will build loyalty and respect. And save yourself a lot of grief in the process.

Do not assume an adversarial relationship with your workers. Management by confrontation is a losing proposition. You may win an occasional battle, but you have my guarantee that you'll lose the war. Above all, do not dismiss your employee's concerns casually. In many cases, if they are calling something to your attention, they have tolerated it for quite a while and have finally worked up the gumption to approach the boss with it. If you disregard or, worse, laugh off a worker's concern, interest, or anxiety, you are asking for trouble. A case in point: One night when I was a dispatcher in Brooklyn, our bureau chief paid us a visit. During a lull in the action, I took the opportunity to point out to him that the Brooklyn Operations Area had no fire exit. Besides the irony involved, there was a real concern for safety. All of the ignition potential—the oil burner, the trash, the kitchen, the computer room—was at the south end of the build-ing, where the only exits were. All of the people were at the north end of the building, where the exits weren't! Since the windows all had gates on them, if something did happen, it seemed that the dispatchers would have to experience some unnecessary risk in order to evacuate the building—if, indeed, they could get out at all.

The chief laughed at me and told me, "If you die here in the line of duty, we'll make sure that you get a flag on your coffin." This was not the answer I expected. The fire service is a results-oriented operation. We solve problems quickly and with intel-ligence. We solve them for thousands of citizens in our protection area whom we've never met, as well as for those people we do know. Therefore, as a dispatcher I expected to have my own concerns addressed with the same degree of respect and se-riousness. When this did not happen, I filed a grievance in accordance with my contract. I needed the protection of my union contract *because my managers would not give me the same protection on their own.*

Needless to say, I got my fire exit. And so did the Bronx Communications Center, which was similarly configured. It cost the department hundreds of hours and thousands of dollars in the time and paper spent in expediting the grievance process. Naturally, they were going to have to pay for the exit doors anyway. But it would have been both financially cheaper and less costly in terms of morale to have said, "Holy Toledo! You're right. It looks like we can't see the forest for the trees—there is a need for fire exits right here in fire communications. I'll get somebody working on that tomorrow morning. We've invested a lot of money in training you guys to be the best and we sure as hell don't want you at risk at work!" Instead of aggravating the situation and incurring unneeded cost, it could have been turned into a very positive thing.

Whether you are working in a unionized situation or not, the same advice applies. Listen! Listen! Listen! Respond to your employees. One of the most frequently ignored areas *in* communications *is* communications. Your employees need a channel to you. If management does not provide one, they will fashion one of their own. Their channel may take the form of increased grievance activity. In the case of non-union operations, it may be evidenced in increased sick leave, more on-the-job injuries, and escalating turnover rates. You must be sensitive to employee needs in order to head off preventable distress. If you are not in tune with their frequency, their signals will start to jam your operations!

And remember that, because they are dispatchers, held to high performance standards by management and themselves, they will expect "the system" to respond to their concerns as quickly as they respond to others' needs. While this position is many times naive or unreasonable, you as a manager of an emergency communications system had better be aware of it.

Even if you are unable to effect some needed change as quickly as your employees may wish, you will want to preempt some of their frustration. By realizing that they have a lower threshold for tolerating the slow-turning wheels of government, you will be able to reduce some of the morale-eroding effects that result from trying to do perfect work in an imperfect system.

Now that you have your people selected, safely housed, efficiently scheduled, and absolutely clear on what they are expected to do and what they can expect from their employer, let's take a look at how they're going to do their jobs.

CHAPTER FIVE

Operations

O PERATIONS IS THE HEART OF emergency communications, the essence of the dispatcher's job—what he does, why he does it, and how he keeps track of it. Operations describes in detail how the dispatcher responds to chaos with orderliness and how he brings structure to the out-of-control situations that are reported to him for resolution.

Let's take a look at three components of the operational structure that dispatchers need to ensure the orderly day-to-day running of your business: paperwork, written guidelines, and quality assurance.

PAPERWORK

Paperwork—forms, records, reports—is often viewed as a necessary evil, but experienced communications professionals regard it as the only way to "cover their flanks." The chapters in this book covering personnel management and scheduling have provided some examples of standard forms necessary for the smooth functioning of these operational areas. There are other uniform means of recording personnel actions (promotions, leave requests, swapping shifts, and so forth) that are not specific to emergency communications operations and may be available through your department. Also, several standardized fire reporting systems, both manual and computer-assisted, are available. Since you work in the fire service and probably read the journals related to the field, you must be using one such system already and are likely aware of some of the others. They all have their advantages and disadvantages. As more departments go to computer-generated data for decision-making support, more software packages will become available for the growing market. But we will not review individual systems here.

The purpose of this section is to get you to think about the kinds of records you need. Do you need all the forms you have? Do you—and this is unfortunately a distinct possibility—need more? (I hear the groans!) Do the forms you currently use meet your needs adequately? You probably have a numbering system for your forms, right? Otherwise, how could you order another gross of TB-86's or ask to have the last 24-hours-worth of BF-219's on your desk in the morning? Well, take your list of forms (you probably have a form number for *that,* too!) and arrange them in order, from the most used to the least used. Then determine the usefulness of those that are least used. The reasons why some of these forms may be gathering dust have more to do with their functions than their usefulness. You hope those fatality reports and multiple-alarm fire to stay right where they are in the file cabinet, buy you'll need them just in case; on the other hand, if your list includes a form used to notify the Civilian Conservation Corps in the event of a forest fire, it's time to review that piece of paper.

On the other end of the scale, look at your most frequently used forms. If you're using them that much, they must be needed, right? Well, probably—but not necessarily. So take a good look. If you decide that a particular form is essential, don't just throw it in the "keep" pile. Review it for possible improvement. A good indicator that something else may be needed on a particular form is how much "marginal" notation is usually found on it. If your multiple-alarm fire forms always have some sideways scribbling on them about which police agency was notified for crowd control, security of the premise, and so forth, then maybe a line for that notification should be included on the form. Another virtue of adding lines or spaces for frequently used notations is that "in-house" abbreviations become less often used. Too often dispatchers fail to realize that their generally low-profile work can suddenly become part of a much scrutinized public record. When folks who are not savvy to the ins and outs of everyday emergency communications try to make sense out of dispatcher jargon that develops outside of the standard guidelines, there is a strong likelihood of misunderstanding and poor communication. To give you an idea of what benefit comes from keeping written communications standardized, I'll tell you about an angry deputy commissioner I once knew.

In many large departments there are lots of deputy commissioners. There might be a designated deputy commissioner for community relations, a deputy commissioner for labor relations, a deputy commissioner for legal affairs, and many others. But the bottom line is that they are most often political appointees who have little or no understanding of the fire service. Before the advent of computer-assisted dispatching in FDNY, the two hundred-or-so FDNY dispatchers scribbled pertinent information on paper "fire tickets." Because the action was sometimes hot and heavy, they resorted to unofficial abbreviations to speed things along a bit. After a particular fire precipitated a lot of political scrutiny, copies of the relevant paperwork, including the fire ticket, were distributed to investigators, among them a deputy commissioner who didn't know an engine from a truck. What he did know was obscenity. And that's what he thought he saw scribbled on the bottom of this fire ticket, because in nice, legible block letters at the very bottom of the ticket was the notation, "FUC 2038." So, he got on his righteous horse and called a few supervisors before he found out that the footnote was not a crude comment but rather a record of the time that the chief placed the

"Fire Under Control"! The new, computer-generated fire reports contain a line that notes the "under control" time—spelled out.

Besides eliminating outdated forms and updating currently useful ones, the emergency communications manager must examine whether or not there is a recurring incidence of unrecorded operational information. It is possible that these "incidental" things could become important. Case in point: When a street or a bridge in your district is closed, or a water main shut off, do you simply call the chief's office of the affected district? Is it possible that a dispatcher on your staff could receive this type of information from the responsible agency and then, distracted by some other business, simply fail to relay it to field forces? Do you "leave a note" for your relief? Do you tape a piece of paper to the radio console? I've often thought that dispatch radio consoles were like refrigerators in the homes of large families: There are always at least a dozen items taped on or stuck on them with magnets! The point is, the communication in a large family is often a lot more confusing and less accurate than can be tolerated by emergency communications professionals.

It may be unlikely that a fire will occur on the very same street that's now closed or where the water main is shut down for maintenance, yet we are in business for the "rare event." It is just good sense to keep a Streets/Bridges Closed log, a Sprinkler System Shutdown log, an Apparatus/Equipment Out of Service log. (The latter should show not only what is out of service but also that all concerned parties have been notified. Frequently, dispatchers take a short view of who needs to know about equipment availability. For instance, if a chief is first on the scene of an accident and is waiting for a first-due truck company to arrive with its power spreader to extricate a victim, he will call for additional aid immediately if he already knows that the tool is out of service.) Where appropriate, keeping a Water Off log is also sound policy (see Figures 5-1 through 5-4). Besides providing a uniform channel of communication for potentially vital data, records of this kind provide an audit trail in the event that a

Figure 5-1
STREETS/BRIDGES CLOSED LOG

Street Closed	Closed Date & Time	Expected Date & Time to be Opened	Source of Info	Company/ Name	Disp. #

Figure 5-2
SPRINKLER SYSTEMS SHUTDOWN LOG

Building Name and Address	Type System	Source of Info	Company Notified/ Name	Date Out	Date In	Disp. #

Figure 5-3

APPARATUS/EQUIPMENT OUT-OF-SERVICE LOG

Apparatus/ Equipment Reported	Date & Time Out of Service	Expected Time Date Back in Service	Source of Info	Company/ Name	Disp. #

Figure 5-4
WATER OFF/UNAVAILABLE LOG

Location	Source/Reason	Date/Time Off/On	Co.	Disp #
Knight's Pond	Low Water	9-20-90 14:15	E173	428
N. Main St.	6" Main Replacement	9-22-90 10:30 ON: 9-23-90 12N	L85	376

Directions: Upon receipt of information that water is OFF/UNAVAILABLE, the dispatcher shall notify the company in whose district the water source lies. Upon receipt of information that the water source is restored, the dispatcher shall enter the date and time ON, making the same notification.

"nobody ever told *me*" situation arises. Going to the log will show you if the information was received by communications personnel and if they relayed it to the affected field forces. It also will give the first clue in tracking down missed messages and will supply the time and date of notification. That in turn will enable you to locate the correct audio tape (it should be a matter of course that *all* official notifications are made on recorded telephones) so that you can make a copy of the actual notification should there be a need to do so. Or you may find that the notification is nowhere on the tape. Either way, you get a better focus on where the responsibility lies.

These are just a few examples of how to approach the overall concern of "forms." Don't be afraid to question the forms and records that "we've always used." If you have an idea for a new form that you think may make things run smoother, don't be afraid to give it a try. Don't write it in stone—give it a trial run—but don't be timid, either. If it doesn't work, send out a memo that says, "Whoops! It didn't work, but at least we'll keep trying to make life easier." You might also solicit suggestions from the troops at that time. In any case, you'll have their respect.

WRITTEN GUIDELINES

Creating written guidelines can be an enormous undertaking. Generally, three basic sets of written guidelines are needed for your emergency communications operation. These are the Communications Center Operations Manual; the Alarm Operations Manual: Signals and Radio; and the Special Situations Operations Manual: Notifications and Procedures.

COMMUNICATIONS CENTER OPERATIONS MANUAL

The Communications Center Operations Manual is usually read by new employees who are orienting to their jobs; by old employees who are studying for promotion; and, most frequently, by all employees who happen to be on duty when something goes wrong!

When putting this manual together (or revising it if you already have one), remember that it is a guideline. You want to give a brief overview of the essential highlights of communications center operations. A dispatcher reading this manual should come away with a good overall understanding of

- the mission of the communications center;
- the design and workings of the plant;
- the plant's equipment;
- dispatcher maintenance functions for that equipment;
- the work flow inside the center;
- the interface between inside plant operations and outside plant (nonfirefighting) operations; and, if applicable,
- the function of a mobile command post or field communications unit in your department.

The mission statement. This, your fundamental statement of purpose, should take into account your operation's emergency and nonemergency functions; the scope of the tasks executed in the communications center; and the manner in which those tasks are to be executed.

The primary mission of every emergency communications center is the receipt and transmission of vital information with speed and accuracy. For a dispatcher to function competently in this mission, he must attend to many tasks and needs. He must keep up-to-date on the characteristics of his protection area: What are the new occupancies? What streets are closed today? What water mains are shut off for repair? He must keep himself in prime condition to meet the demands that are made of him (get sleep before the night tours, no hangovers, etc.). A comprehensive mission statement will let the dispatcher know just how important he is to the optimal functioning of the unit. It will emphasize that job preparedness is his duty not only to the public he protects but also to his fellow employees.

Although the public is the principal beneficiary of the dispatcher's expertise, the field forces rely on it as well. The dispatcher is responsible for getting them the most accurate information in the fastest way possible so that they can get to the right place with a good idea of what to expect when they get there. The dispatcher also has an obligation to be aware of any resources within or outside the department that the field forces may someday urgently need (a helicopter, a front-end loader, shoring timbers) and know how to deliver those resources to the emergency scene. There is a duty to pay attention to the units in the field at all times—particularly when you *haven't* heard from them. The dispatcher is well-known as the link between the public and protection; he is also the lifeline between the field forces and additional help. An officer in any sort of distress (an apparatus accident, hostile citizens, a collapse with firefighters trapped) reaches first for his handset. Your dispatchers had better be there to respond when he calls—or be astute enough to realize when he hasn't called and is overdue.

The mission statement also should stress the obligation each employee has to the department and the municipality to conduct himself in a way that brings no discredit to his employer. Sometimes this can be more difficult to keep in mind when dealing with the less urgent aspects of emergency communications work. Like it or not, your operation is viewed by the public as a reliable source of information, and you will receive nonemergency calls that may seem rather urgent to the callers. Most dispatchers get a good feeling from the reassurances they give to callers after earth tremors, sonic booms, and fireworks, yet sometimes it's hard to be courteous with folks who want to use you for your street index or for other nonemergency matters. Your dispatchers should frame their responses in such situations by viewing the calls with pride rather than annoyance. Obviously, these callers have faith that you will be there to answer their calls, that you will be able to give them accurate information and refer them to the proper places. The dispatcher has a duty to deal professionally with these calls as well as with the emergencies.

These obligations make up, in most basic form, the mission of the communications center—your mission. Construct the mission statement in a way that meets your needs, but remember the bases we've just touched. Your mission statement will prepare the dispatcher to go into the rest of the Communications Center Operations Manual with a greater sense of the whys of his job and with an understanding of how communications operations come together.

Design and workings of the plant. This section of the manual should supply the dispatcher with a plant floor plan to review, a breakdown of the plant's component areas (operating area, sometimes called the alarm room; terminal room, where incoming fire alarm circuits terminate and burnout protection equipment is located; and power plant), and a listing of the personnel who staff the operation, with their phone numbers.

Plant equipment. Include the standard radio equipment, telephones, tape recording systems (again, for the protection of your personnel, I strongly advise that you record *every* telephone and radio position in the communications center), alarm receipt boards, running or status boards, CAD-related equipment (CRTs, printers), and any other "stuff" your operation relies on to provide emergency communications. You can move these ideas around the manual in any fashion that strikes you as orderly and sensible. You may wish to list the power plant under "design and workings of the plant" but explain its operation and maintenance in more detail in the "equipment" section. Or you may wish to have a separate section set aside simply for the power plant. Just as your manuals will be guidelines for your dispatchers, this section is a guideline for you. Like the rest of this book, it is designed to help you look at all the possibilities, to think of things you may otherwise have forgotten, and to give suggestions—not to dictate. Good suggestions sometimes never get implemented but nevertheless provide stimulus for some productive thought and action. Feel free to run with your own good judgment!

Dispatcher maintenance functions for equipment. This section can range from a listing of routine circuit testing (ground testing, open circuit testing, looking for crossed circuits, etc.) to refilling printer paper to precautions when working around keyboards and CRTs.

The routine for replacing the 24-hour recording tapes and for logging reel numbers off and on should be outlined here. The number of tapes with which your center should normally operate depends on how long your jurisdiction wishes to preserve evidence. Usually, if anything out of the ordinary is going to develop from a particular operation, the supervisor on duty either will be able to sense this or will be notified by the field commander involved. In these cases the tape is usually pulled out of the rotation and kept aside for the investigating authorities. It's a good idea to hold a tape of communications from an incident in which there has been a fatality, a complaint of delayed response, or any kind of a telephoned threat. Experience shows that these are going to be requested for further examination.

Sometimes the request for a tape is unanticipated and does not arise until months after the event. Check with your local counsel as to how long you should hold each tape, and always err on the side of conservatism. The procedure for responding to requests for tapes should be outlined in your Special Situations Operations Manual.

The how-to's of originating work orders for plumbing, electrical work, and so on should also be noted here in the dispatcher maintenance section. Naturally, it's most often the people using the place and its equipment every day who will find if something is wrong with it. You may want to consider including some maintenance rounds whereby a dispatcher and a supervisor actually walk around the place with a checklist to make sure that things are in working order.

Work flow inside the center. As a general approach to illustrating the work flow, it's probably easiest to present a simple narrative of how an alarm is received, processed, and dispatched. This way you can describe each function and show how they integrate with one another, while giving the novice dispatcher an overall sense of what happens to his work when it is elsewhere in the work flow. A chart showing the many possible sources and outcomes is also useful here (see Figure 5-5).

Interface between inside and outside plant (nonfirefighting) operations. If you have not already done so, you will want to cover the terminal room in some detail. Make sure to include how to make substitutions to spare feeders, how to transfer conductors, and what communications protocol is followed with the outside plant personnel during these operations. The function of protection devices that guard against burnout from lightning or from contact of alarm circuits with powerlines also should be addressed here.

Function of a mobile command post or field communications unit. Many smaller departments have no need for such a unit. In some cases, a county or combined-agency mobile communications center is used. If you use a field communications unit, make sure that its function is clearly understood by all. Generally, such a unit is used at extended and large-scale operations. It serves as the conduit for all communications regarding the various needs at the scene. Field communications personnel monitor many aspects of the operation, including arrival and placement of units at the scene, status reports, interagency communications, and on-scene portable radio communications.

ALARM OPERATIONS MANUAL: SIGNALS AND RADIO

This is a basic "how-to" on your day-to-day workings of the communications network. It should include all your ten-code signals. Different regions have standardized ten-codes, and for the sake of clarity and consistency you'll probably want to keep

Figure 5-5
ALARM PROCESSING WORKFLOW

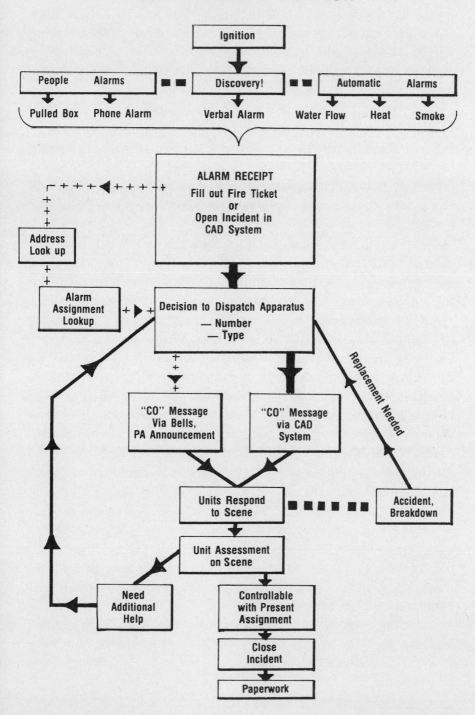

in line with your neighbors. Most ten-codes have conversational utility, while others can summon additional assistance, accelerate states of readiness, or initiate preplanned courses of action. They can trigger such diverse items as opening county shelters during widespread disaster, "move-ups" or relocation of emergency equipment into stripped areas, and halting all nonessential radio traffic during busy periods.

This manual should cover your radio protocol on a wide range of items such as call letters and station identification, routine radio contact requirements, courtesy, technical means of securing communications, and the proper way to intrude with an urgent message, just to name a few. How to tone out units and announcements should be defined, as should radio and plectron testing.

The Alarm Operations Manual should stress the importance of uniformity in communications technique, something that must be consciously developed, strengthened, and reinforced. Uniformity in technique is one of the tools at the dispatcher's disposal for maintaining control of diverse emergency situations through his contact with a wide variety of individuals (see Figure 5-6). The least controllable variable is the civilian, who may be hysterical, ignorant, drunk, lying, hostile, arrogant, mistaken, speaking a foreign language, or simply too talkative; the most controllable variables are members of the department. The need for uniformity—being the one constant in the tornado of chaos— is obvious in the case communications with civilians, yet even during communications with department members the dispatcher will have to work at control. Changing shifts in the field and in the communications center make it so.

If you make a lot of routine announcements, you may want to include their formats as samples in your Alarm Operations Manual. In some areas, these announcements include weather forecasts; road, traffic, or brush conditions; school closings or delays; and training bulletins.

As you prepare to write or revise the Alarm Operations Manual, you may find that many operational elements either are

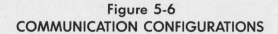

Figure 5-6
COMMUNICATION CONFIGURATIONS

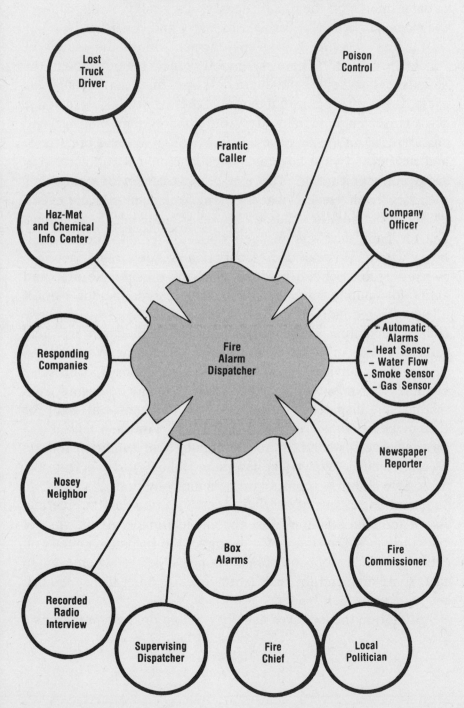

not written down anywhere or have become lost. This is a good opportunity to bring all your radio operations and procedures up to date, smooth off the rough edges, and give all your dispatchers the means for communicating effectively and consistently.

I'll leave you to your own judgment about the matter of "radio discipline." There is obviously no question about the seriousness of the life-and-death decisions made in this business every day. It is recognized that one of the ways of taking the edge off a tense job is to allow for some expressions of pride and camaraderie on the airwaves. It is a matter of local preference and custom as to just how much free-lancing will be tolerated in radio communications. The use of nicknames for companies ("Calling Triple Deuce" when looking for Engine 222, for example) is something that can be okay in nonemergency situations. But the habit develops and gets carried over into the hot-and-heavy action. This can cause confusion and delay, and therefore is not a recommended practice. Straying outside the prepared script for routine announcements is a less dangerous way of allowing some individual expression, and it can go a long way toward cementing useful bonds between dispatchers and field forces. A case in point would be the Dangerous Weather Advisory. After advising units to put in tire chains and exercise caution when responding to, operating at, and returning from alarms, one dispatcher further advised, "It's not a fit night for man or beast out there—be careful guys!" Another helpful dispatcher gave firsthand, up-to-the-minute road condition reports by announcing, "We've just have some fellows come in from the West Side and they report extreme icing conditions."

Another example of unofficial messages, the holiday greeting, has in some jurisdictions now become legitimate. At the start of the Christmas Day tours, for example, the dispatcher reads an official greeting from the commissioner, chief, or whomever. In fact, some areas go for real "showtime" and broadcast a taped message from their leader.

Humor on the airwaves usually is heard only when there is a

seasoned dispatcher on duty. You have to be relaxed and confident to be spontaneously humorous on the air, and that usually gives the manager a built-in check on when the humor is used: A veteran dispatcher will not kid around when the chips are down. For all "unauthorized transmissions," the productivity/deviance ratio is a good rule of thumb. The more productive a dispatcher is, the more deviance from the norm is tolerated. A goldbrick gets no slack. And in no case should the completely outrageous—such as the fellow who at midnight announced, "We now conclude our broadcast day"—be tolerated.

SPECIAL SITUATIONS OPERATIONS MANUAL: NOTIFICATIONS AND PROCEDURES

There are routine alarms and not-so-routine alarms. For fire service personnel the "routine" alarms may be automobile fires, food-on-the-stove fires, brushfires, defective oil burners, and clogged incinerators. We become more comfortable and proficient with these alarms the more we handle them. But we also have to be able to deal with "special" situations that we must identify and plan for.

What makes a situation special? It is most often the gravity or the scope of the event: Plane crashes, ship fires, multiple fatalities, hazardous-materials exposures, bomb threats, and so forth are obviously beyond the ordinary. Sometimes the special nature of a situation is a function of a political reality: An auto fire takes on added significance when the auto belongs to the governor! In any case, experienced dispatchers usually know when they have a special situation.

The purpose of this manual is to direct your dispatchers on handling unusual events. These directions usually involve automatic responses of special units not routinely included in an alarm assignment and notifications of higher-ups and other interested agencies.

There is a challenge to writing any of these manuals. You want to be able to anticipate any operational communications need your dispatchers may face. Additionally, when putting together a Special Situations Operations Manual, you must anticipate just how special a situation has to be before you wake up a deputy mayor, civil defense coordinator, or fire marshal. I remember an incident involving a new dispatcher that typifies what I'm talking about. Usually, you start your new dispatchers off in a "paperwork" position; he or she holds down the final stop in the routing of the alarm through the communications center. This position involves logging alarms, making notifications, answering inquiries about current and recent alarms, and generally tidying up the loose paper ends. While this is not as exciting as answering fire phones or talking on the radio, it does develop the dispatcher's sense of what information is needed on a fire ticket and why. The benefit of this paperwork experience will show later when he is able to ask callers and field units the right questions spontaneously because he knows what will be needed later on for reports and investigators.

As is often the case, this rookie dispatcher was quite a student of the regulations. He diligently recorded alarm activity, called the American Red Cross to relocate burned-out residents, notified the water department of broken hydrants, requested police for traffic control, made sure that salt spreaders were on hand to deal with slippery roads after the fire department had extinguished car fires, and generally slogged away at the nuts and bolts of his paperwork position—that is, until the supervising dispatcher received an irate call from the fire marshal's office, saying, "What the hell do we care if there's a car fire at three in the morning if there's not a bomb or a body involved?" The supervisor, in turn, jumped on his paperwork man, who had called the marshal's office three times that shift to notify him of car fires! The rookie, shocked at this turn of events, innocently pointed out to his boss that the regulations demanded that the fire marshal's office be notified in the event of a "transportation fire." Since car fires were counted under the statistical category of "transportation," it seemed only logical and correct to make the notification. Needless to say, the rules were made more specific regarding *public* transportation fires!

I've already recommended that you review all of your operations forms annually. Yearly review of your operating manuals is at least as important. Had that review been going on in the case noted above, everybody (or at least more people than just the rookie) would have been familiar enough with both the rules and the standard procedure to realize that there was a discrepancy that needed resolution. When you review notifications procedures, make it a point to call or write to the designated recipient of the notification. Let him know what to expect and when to expect it. Whether you call or write depends on several considerations. The size of your department is one. If yours is a small operation and you regularly work closely with all the participants involved, a call should be sufficient. If you have a larger operation, or if the history of communication between your department and the intended notification has been strained, take the time to write a letter. You might even want to cover your flanks with a return envelope and a confirmation form (see Figure 5-7 on page 130). In this way a lot of potential disputes are pre-empted. You may also find that a lot of folks who traditionally have been on your notifications list no longer have an interest in being there or have delegated the duty to others in their agencies. In addition to an annual review, it is also a good idea to keep in touch with promotions and appointments in cooperating agencies. A letter to a new county commissioner can congratulate her on her new position, will let her know that she's on the county's disaster notifications list, and also very clearly give the message that you're on the ball—which won't hurt if you need to swing a budget request someday!

If you're starting your Special Situations Manual from scratch, you may find it easiest to divide the task into two categories: Why? and Who? Take the time to sit down with your

Figure 5-7
FORM MEMO FOR CONFIRMATION OF
NOTIFICATION LIST INCLUSION/EXCLUSION

FIRE DEPARTMENT
CONFIRMATION OF NOTIFICATION LIST STATUS

I, _____, understand that I am currently on the Fire Department notification list for the following events:

☐ Multiple-alarm incidents

☐ Building collapse

☐ Hazardous-materials spill

☐ Civilian death

☐ Uniformed death

☐ Uniformed injury

☐ Suspicious fire

☐ Other: _____

Please check all that apply:

☐ I wish to be kept on the notification list.

☐ Please make note that the following person in our department will now be receiving such notification:

☐ Please remove my name from your notification list.

☐ Please make the following changes in the circumstances in which I wish to be notified (make additions or deletions here):

Sincerely,

SIGNATURE

dispatchers and compile a list of why they have called for extra resources and/or manpower in extraordinary events. There are the more obvious categories of multiple-alarm fires, hazardous-materials incidents, and multicasualty incidents. And there are the less frequent but still large-scale operations such as derailments; water main and gas line breaks; building collapse; apparatus accidents; airport, bridge, tunnel, and marine disasters; bomb threats; explosions of various types; and disruption of fire alarm service.

The formulation of specific emergency response plans preempts the ad-lib response situation at times when all the bases need to be covered. These plans clearly point out everybody's tasks—both in the field and in the communications center—when faced with disaster. Emergency response plans afford you the opportunity to coordinate multiple public and private resources in advance. They also call for drills so that lessons can be learned from mistakes without dire consequences. The drill will help you to experience in a concrete way what demands will be made on your system and its people. Try out phone numbers, start up back-up generators, become familiar with less frequently used mutual-aid agreements. If there are any holes in your plan, you will be able to address them as you revise and update your Special Situations Manual. Time and again, we have seen the payoff—in air crashes, earthquakes, and chemical spills—for emergency response drills. Make certain that your manual is quite clear on the roles of your dispatchers in these incidents so that the full benefit of such planning can be realized.

Beyond these incidents are those that are of a smaller scale operationally but are quite significant nonetheless. These include deaths and injuries; fires in public mailboxes; reported thefts at fires; relocation of residents burned out of their homes; fires in publicly owned buildings; and fires involving utility service shut-off.

After you ascertain the why's, take a look at the who's to contact in special situations. You can further divide this group into "Responders" and "Notifications." Responders include people and units both inside and outside the department who *must* go to the scene. These calls are made before notifications, who do not necessarily respond to the incident. When you list your responders, prioritize the order in which they are called. For instance, for a four-alarm fire at night, a searchlight truck would be called before a canteen unit. A mask service/air supply unit would go before the fire marshal. In many cases, of course, there will be emergency calls that will intervene in the scheduled priority. The sudden discovery of chemical drums at a warehouse fire will necessitate a call to a clearinghouse for emergency chemical information to get an interpretation of number codes on the containers and information about the contents' potential danger and burn characteristics. So remember that the Special Situations Manual should guide the dispatcher's actions, not supplant his judgment. If a dispatcher elects to go outside the normal order of things in a certain situation, he will usually have a good reason for doing so.

On occasion, your department will have need for resources from the private sector of the community. These can include items such as cranes, helicopters, heavy equipment for tunneling and earth moving, blasting supplies, and shoring timbers. Clearly, when private resources are concerned it is more difficult to keep notification numbers up-to-date, especially for non-business hours. Unless yours is a small-town jurisdiction in which everybody knows where to find a bulldozer operator at two in the morning, I recommend that you review this list of contacts every six months.

Notifications are made to many different people and agencies for many different reasons. They do not always result in somebody actually going to the scene of the incident and are, therefore, of a lesser priority. Here again, however, the dispatcher must use his judgment. If yours is a medium-sized city where the mayor's office has traditionally been notified on all fires of a third alarm or greater, the importance of notification depends on who the mayor is (and sometimes where in the polls he is). If it is simply a courtesy notification so that he can review it on his morning report of overnight events in his city, then it can be made later in the incident. If your mayor either is a fire buff or figures that his appearance at the scene will give him a welcome opportunity to display his leadership qualities in front of the local TV minicams, then a timely notification of the mayor's office is in order.

In the cases of both those notified to respond and those who are notified for informational purposes, you most definitely should keep a log of the communications involved. Your log should indicate who was reached, how the person was reached, the time of the contact, and the dispatcher making the contact. If there was no contact made, this should also be noted, along with the time and means by which the contact was attempted. Additionally, your log should have a "comments" section just in case somebody offers one! (See Figure 5-8.) Ideally, a two-part form makes for a good log sheet; one part will be attached to the fire report and the other will be filed at the communications center.

Finally, since special situations almost always call for some kind of review, your manual should cover the procedure by which requests for audio tapes are made and the circumstances under which a dispatcher can release tapes to a requesting authority. The tape log should have a space where a dispatcher can indicate if the chief, fire marshal, state police, county prosecutor—or whoever—has either requested the tape or held it out of the regular tape rotation (see Figure 5-9). The tape log shows what reels were recording at what time. Always allow for more reels than days in a month since investigators may wish to take a tape at any time, creating a situation in which a day's work is contained on more than one 24-hour tape.

QUALITY ASSURANCE

Now that you have all your paperwork in place, properly supporting your day-to-day operations, you can begin to use it for

Figure 5-8
NOTIFICATION LOG

MULTIPLE-ALARM NOTIFICATION LOG

Date:
Address:
Box Number:

Notifications: Person/Office	Times: Transmitted				
	2nd Alarm	3rd Alarm	4th Alarm	5th Alarm	Under Control
	18:37	18:45	18:49		
Shift Commander (Foley)	18:40 (Davis)				
Deputy Chief Grimm	18:41 (Davis)	18:46 (Johnson)	18:49 (via radio)		
Police Dept. Disp. #428	18:42 (Davis)				
Ambulance Disp. #105		18:48 (Johnson)			
Press Relations Officer (Carr)		18:50 (Johnson)			
Mayor's Office (notified Spec. ass't. Rondo)			18:51 (Johnson)		

TAPE LOG

Date	Tape #	Time on	Time off	Initials	Comments

another important activity. You spent a lot of time and money on developing the forms and guidelines. Certainly, the importance of the public safety activity supported in part by that paperwork justifies the investment. However, you can get even more mileage out of the paperwork by using it for quality assurance (QA) activities.

You may be thinking, What is quality assurance and why do I need it in an emergency communications system? After all, this isn't a factory where I'm producing parts that can be examined for defects—this is the fire service! The fact is, while your communications center may not be a factory, you do "produce" something there: *service*. At first glance, QA looks to most line troops like just another paper exercise. It's certainly not something you *have* to do. In fact, it's rarely done in emergency communications beyond measuring response times and investigating errors. So what's the point? Properly presented, QA can be a major source of efficiency and pride in your department. Rather than being keyed to negative events, a good QA program examines the processes that yield positive outcomes so that such results can be achieved again. Quality assurance is a structured way of asking two questions. Most basic is the question, Are we really as good as we think we are?

Now, before you go and formally ask this of your workers, you must be aware that the way you present the question can make all the difference in the world. After all, it can appear that you have doubts about their work, and that is not the point in asking the question. Therefore, in order to properly focus your QA energy toward ensuring a positive outcome, it is better to ask a more involved question first: How can we get better? By starting from this point, you will be accentuating the positive, capitalizing on your dispatchers' positive attitude toward delivery of service and accepting as a given that your staff already is good. You will also get the answer to the other question without casting any doubt about the current level of performance.

Before you can devise a plan to improve performance, you

have to ascertain a baseline. In setting this benchmark, you may discover that all aspects of your dispatching operation are not exactly up to par. Alone, this discovery can be a blow to morale. Indeed, when people who think they've been doing a fine job find that they have been missing something, it can be downright depressing. However, when the deficiencies are noted as part of a plan for improvement, the attention can be placed more on the desired future goal than on the undesirable past mistakes.

Once a baseline is established, you'll have to determine a means to measure performance. Before you start devising elaborate new methods of checking work, a good beginning is to take some of your existing paperwork and track it. For instance, retrieve your safety checklists and track how long it takes to correct a noted unsafe condition. If it took an average of six weeks to correct a problem in the first quarter of the year but now, in the third quarter, it takes only a month, this shows improvement. Examine your Notifications logs. If your multiple-alarm fires require ten notifications and your review shows that an average of only seven are being made, this is obviously an area for improvement.

Whenever possible, involve your dispatchers in the operational performance reviews; it will have a beneficial effect on their future practice by giving them a more global perspective of what they do. And it should be made clear from the start that this is not a "witch hunt." Be sensible enough to realize that the data accumulated from your initial performance measurements is only a starting point and not something on which to draw conclusions or lay blame. Take the case in which not all of the multiple-alarm notifications are being made: Closer scrutiny may reveal that one or two of the notifications are consistently unreachable, through no lack of effort on the dispatchers' part.

Besides direct operational applications, QA also has obvious administrative uses. Tracking sick days and on-the-job injuries historically has been used to measure a unit's overall effectiveness. Like the paper reviews already mentioned, this is retrospective research. The other mode in which QA can be pursued is concurrent review. This is a far more expensive means of measuring effectiveness because it involves an uninvolved party making and recording observations of dispatching events as they happen. The most common of these exercises are "time and motion" studies, in which an observer with a stopwatch breaks down the dispatch process into individual components and clocks each of them. The object is to reduce inefficient motion and accelerate delivery of service.

Another, less frequently used study that requires an observer in the communications center is the "workload multiplier" study. This study is usually implemented after somebody has complained about service. It could happen like this: The mayor's wife, driving down Main Street, sees a car fire. Being a good citizen, she pulls over at a pay phone and tells the operator she wants to report a fire. The operator connects her to the communications center, where the phone rings twelve times before somebody gets around to helping Mrs. Mayor. Outraged, she tells hubby at the dinner table that the local municipal services are something less than up to snuff. His Honor gets on the horn to the fire chief, who rattles enough cages to get an immediate report of exactly what the hell *was* going on in the communications center at two o'clock on a sunny Sunday afternoon.

The report comes back: Between one-thirty and two-thirty on Sunday afternoon, there were exactly three alarms transmitted— a "food on the stove," a "defective oil burner," and "Mrs. Mayor's car fire." To handle the alarms in this city of 150,000 souls was the usual complement of three on-duty dispatchers. The chief knows that this data will not float on its own. When he brings back this report of sparse alarm activity, he had also better bring back a sacrificial lamb to appease His Honor. He orders the audio tape to his office pronto so he can find out which of the three dispatchers is not on the tape. After his investigation determines which of these slugs was reading comic books instead of answering phones, he will take disciplinary action, which he hopes will be sufficient enough to keep the mayor out of his shop, assert his leadership, and send a message to the troops.

However, when the chief settles in to listen to the tape, he is astounded to hear all three dispatchers on the phone before, during, and after the time that Mrs. Mayor was doing her duty. How can this be? There were only three alarms! Of course, if the chief was more in touch with his operation, he would be less eager to find a scapegoat. He would know that there is a big difference between what traditionally and erroneously has been used as a measure of dispatcher workload—alarms transmitted—and the actual amount of work that dispatchers are doing every day. When he listens to the tape, he hears the dispatchers take a total of 23 calls for what turned out to be a smoky defective oil burner in a high-rise apartment building. He hears an out-of-town truck driver calling to find out where a particular street is, a newspaper reporter calling for an update on last night's alarms, a girlfriend looking for an off-duty dispatcher, the water department letting the fire department know that they could not provide any water pressure today on Eleventh Avenue due to a main break, a hospital security guard reporting that a fire drill would be held at three o'clock, an engine officer calling to get correct "out" times for runs earlier in the shift, six people calling to report open fire hydrants, somebody looking for a free smoke detector, three calls reporting smoke from a restaurant that turned out to be the "food on the stove," and of course, Mrs. Mayor. Forty calls. Three alarms. With the exception of the lost girlfriend, all the calls were more or less legitimate, even if most were not emergencies. At the time Mrs. Mayor phoned there were seven calls clustered in thirty seconds. You could hear the other phones ringing in the background while the dispatchers spoke. Actually, the guys that the chief was looking to hang did a pretty good job in sorting through the calls; they weren't rude or abrupt with any of the callers and they still got the alarms transmitted in an acceptable amount of time.

Suddenly, it dawns on the chief that he may not have a real

good handle on the volume of data being processed in his communications center. What he needs, he decides, is a way to quantify *everything* that's happening there—not just alarms transmitted. So, in one fashion or another, he sets out to develop a workload multiplier for his department—a factor that can be used with the existing statistic of alarms transmitted to give a reasonably accurate measurement of how much work his dispatchers are doing. He now knows that, for whatever reason the phones are ringing, the dispatchers cannot prioritize the calls and match them up to available resources until they have at least answered them!

Of course, one of the ways that many departments have dealt with this problem is to publish two telephone numbers, one for emergencies and one for routine business. In this way, the callers are actually prioritizing their concerns to some degree before the dispatcher gets to them. If both the emergency and routine phones ring simultaneously, we know who's going to wait. Had they both come in on one line, there's a fifty–fifty chance that the emergency waits while the dispatcher takes enough time to make the preliminary determination that it's okay to put the routine call on hold.

Nonetheless, you do want to know exactly what kind of volume your dispatchers are handling. The workload multiplier will give you a reasonable estimate. To formulate the workload multiplier, assign an uninvolved observer to record everything the dispatchers do. Because you want your data to be as reliable as possible, I strongly recommend that you do not use an off-duty dispatcher for this task. I can hear the defensive cries now: What's the matter, don't you trust us? The answer is no, I don't! It's not that I expect the off-duty dispatcher to inflate statistics to secure his job or show the city how much work he's doing. Quite to the contrary, I don't trust the average off-duty dispatcher to record *enough* of the work that his fellow dispatchers do. I've seen it before: A dispatcher takes an in-service call from a company that's been out of service for a few minutes for an oil change, or whatever. Then he doesn't mark it down on the work-load tally sheet. "What was that call?" I ask. "Oh, Engine 201 just went back in service; it was only out a few minutes," he replies. Because this is only one of literally thousands of calls that the dispatcher takes each year—and probably one of the least significant when compared to some of the exciting and emotional life-and-death conversations he has had in the past—it does not seem important enough to be tallied. However, the dispatcher is not answering a fire phone while he's taking the in-service call. No call, even a wrong number, is too insignificant to be tallied when you are formulating a workload multiplier. That's why you have to have a recorder who is not familiar with the surroundings and will not become lax in tallying calls. An out-sider will not be susceptible to assigning priorities to calls sub-consciously, thus losing them for the total. So your recorder will count not only alarms but administrative messages, referrals to other agencies, informational calls, duplicate calls for the same event, notifications, and, yes, wrong numbers.

After your scorekeeper has registered all the various dispatcher phone actions, turn your attention to all the other tasks your dispatcher may be required to perform. Equipment tests, custodial duties, and receptionist tasks (handing out applications for burn permits, for example) are all dispatcher actions. Take the sum of all these dispatcher actions and compare them with your faithfully kept statistic of alarms transmitted to arrive at your workload multiplier. The formula is as follows:

$$\frac{\text{DISPATCHER ACTIONS}}{\text{ALARMS TRANSMITTED}} = \text{WORKLOAD MULTIPLIER}$$

Be prepared to be somewhat startled by the results. A study conducted more than a decade ago in New York City showed that FDNY dispatchers received an average of 17.55 calls of various types for every alarm they transmitted.

There are many factors influencing variations in the workload multiplier. These factors will show great divergence between adjacent jurisdictions in a comparative study. If yours is a town where folks tend to take great interest in the community, you can expect that you will be hearing from them frequently. If you are protecting a larger city where there is a more impersonal atmosphere, you may be hearing from the public less often. If yours is a jurisdiction in which the fire department is known for being helpful in all sorts of nonemergent, "cat-in-the-tree" situations, or if other agencies are known as less responsive than your own, the number of calls will probably be rather large, thus increasing your workload multiplier.

Consider the weather when factoring a workload multiplier. Regionally, there is no consistent expected outcome for a certain type of weather so, once again, it comes down to knowing your area of protection. The same weather can produce opposite effects on workload, depending on when and where that weather is occurring. Areas that have large tracts of land susceptible to brushfires traditionally augment forces when there is a high Brushfire Spread Index. A good rainfall in these areas generally can be expected to lower demands on fire protection resources. However, in moderately settled areas that same rainfall can have exactly the opposite effect as you experience an increase in service demand for events such as flooding, powerlines down, and water/electrical emergencies inside buildings. Other extrinsic factors that can produce a predictable trend in alarm activity are seasonal population changes in resort areas; major sporting events such as the World Series, Super Bowl, or a championship boxing match, which seem to depress alarm activity; and—yes, that's right—the full moon!

I recommend that you gather your workload multiplier data over an extended period of time, or during several time periods at different points in the year, so as to even out the statistical "blips" that can occur. I also recommend that this data be revalidated every couple of years to keep up with changes in your protection area. (We will discuss this further in Chapter Eight: "Planning.")

So how does the workload multiplier connect with your overall concerns for quality assurance? For one thing, the results of QA studies support organizational decision making. Without a workload multiplier, you are minus up-to-the-minute data and your decisions may be suspect. Consequently, you can have the best QA program in the world and still not have a handle on what kind of work it is that your people are doing. For another thing, in emergency communications especially, one of the primary forces that dilutes the quality of service provided is insufficient staffing. The workload multiplier's primary use is in determining the appropriateness of your staffing levels. If you find that your operation's workload multiplier is high, you may even want to take things a bit further than increasing staff: You may want to rewrite job descriptions so that any dispatcher tasks not directly related to emergency communications are eliminated. This may mean hiring a contract cleaning service rather than expecting dispatchers to "police the area." It may mean hiring a receptionist so that the dispatcher does not have time-consuming, face-to-face nonemergency public contact. Or, if it is simply impossible to afford a receptionist, it may mean limiting the hours during which members of the public can come to the public safety building for their permits. In any case, when the need for change is recognized, it will result in better service to the people you serve.

As you can see from the brief overview that this chapter has provided, the topic of operations is both broad and essential. It is a major challenge in the face of so much routine business in emergency communications to keep your dispatching staff up to par in this area, yet failure to do so compromises your mission: speedy and accurate communication of data necessary for the protection of life and property.

CHAPTER SIX

Training

S O FAR, WE'VE CHOSEN the right place, equipped it with the right stuff, staffed it with the right people, and scheduled them at the right times. We have made an effort to do the right thing by our folks and we have outlined what it is we expect them to do. Now, to bring it all together the right way, we need to address a much neglected area in emergency communications: training.

Training? Yeah, we got training. Let's see, we sent a guy to a state conference last spring, right? Or was it the spring before last?

State and regional conferences are terrific at times. They allow you to get together with other people in the field and exchange ideas about your profession. They also enable you to attract experts from outside your area to make presentations to your group. On the down side, big conferences cost money and take time. Not very many departments have big budgets for travel time, replacement labor costs for conference attendees, meals, and lodging. Even if the money is available you must always bear in mind that no matter how good the conference presenters are, the value to your department is limited by the judgment, understanding, and interpersonal communications skills of the representative you send. After all, it's up to him to bring the information back to the rest of your department as it was presented. It's a nice break in the routine and certainly a morale booster to be able to send someone to a conference. But it's not always easy to convince the taxpayers that sending Dispatcher Brennan to the Ninth Annual Hawaiian Antenna Conference will bring immeasurable benefit to the people of rural Idaho!

Sure we have training. Everybody gets a manual when they come on the job.

Training does *not* end with orientation. If you have read this far in the book, you know that the manual itself should have gone through some changes over the years, if for no other reason than to reflect the changes in the fire service at large. Besides the changes brought on by technological advances, there are the changes that have taken place in your area of protection. The book you handed out to your dispatchers when they were filling out their insurance enrollment cards probably belongs in a fire museum somewhere, not in a place of reference for training purposes.

How much training can you do? The job hasn't changed since I joined the department.

Yes, Virginia, there are still people who think and talk this way. Not to belabor a point made before in this book, but the fire service is not a static entity. If it is to be effective in its mission, it must be a dynamic organization responding to the everpresent changes in the community it protects. There are plenty of folks reading this now who can remember a time when the term "haz mat" was unheard of in the fire service, when "computer-assisted dispatch," "rapid water," and "mobile data transmission" were science fiction. Today's emergency communications personnel must be fluent in today's protection language. A dispatcher who works in proximity to a nuclear power plant had better know what an "exposure plume pathway" is. The last ten years' advances in on-the-scene emergency medicine alone would fill volumes. So the idea that this is the same old job is truly denying some realities. The spirit, you hope, may be the same. The positive attitude toward the delivery of service may still be present. But the tools, needed knowledge, and demands for service are constantly changing.

You want me to spend time and money on training? Let me tell you something: These guys know the job!"

Time, yes. You absolutely must spend time on training. Money, not necessarily. Aside from keeping in touch with the evolution of the profession through purchase and reading of professional journals, your training budget does not have to bust the bank in order for you to have an effective training program.

As far as "these guys know the job" goes, any guy who *does* know the job will tell you how much more there is that he feels he needs to know. The folks who feel that they know it all—the ones who become complacent about the routine aspects of their jobs and let that laziness carry over into the rest of their work—are the people who will make the killer mistakes.

So what is training? In its simplest definition, it's preparing to do the job. Therefore, to organize an effective training program you have to analyze what it takes to do the job. To start, you can review earlier chapters in this book. All of the needed components for productive job performance have been addressed. You can then break your training program into categories:
  • familiarization with expected duties;
  • knowledge of the equipment, both in the communications center and in the field;
  • knowledge of the techniques of emergency communications operations;
  • knowledge of the procedures and when they are used;
  • knowledge of your jurisdiction and its protection needs;

• ability to assess the working environment of the communications center and knowledge of how to effect changes in that environment when indicated; and finally, in order to help ensure the optimal functioning of the personnel who bring all of these parts together,

• awareness of stress—how to manage it, recognize its sources, and respond to it. This is a key part of an effective training program.

It's advisable to set aside some regular staff time to examine at least one of these important issues each week. Let's look at them now and determine how to ensure competency in each.

FAMILIARIZATION WITH EXPECTED DUTIES

Naturally, the starting place here is the job description. Remember that you are determining whether or not a particular task is within the dispatcher's duties. How to do that task is something else. The focus here is on making sure that the dispatcher does not either turn away from or fail to do something that you expect him to do.

Additionally, you don't want him spending time doing things that are not part of his job. For one thing, the dispatcher is a person who must be there when you need him, and you cannot predict when that will be. If he is distracted from his primary mission by becoming involved in matters that are not part of his job, it may add to your response time—something that you simply cannot tolerate. It helps to recognize that the boring down times between alarms are when the temptation to branch out into other endeavors is greatest. I remember a situation in which a communications center was undergoing renovation and there were several contractors running around the place. One of our dispatchers, who did a fair amount of electrical work in his off time, noticed what he felt was a better way to run cable across the room to another. He got involved with the electrical subcontractor on the renovation (who was getting paid a decent sum to do this job *himself*) and was standing in the middle of the operations room holding a bunch of cable over his head when the fire phones started ringing. His electrician "partner" was yelling at him to hold on for "just one more minute"; of course, it has to be presumed that the citizen on the fire phone doesn't have that one more minute to give!

Another reason you don't want him involved in activities that aren't part of his job is that you can reasonably assume he has not been trained to do them. Therefore, if you look the other way while he does a bit of jerry-rigged electrical work, for instance, you are accepting some liability for the consequences if something goes wrong. If there is reason to make certain kinds of modifications, then have a qualified, insured person do the job.

For unionized operations, there is always the possibility that by depending on dispatchers to perform nondispatching duties you may find yourself looking at charges of demanding "out-of-title" work from them. You are also vulnerable to charges from the folks whose job it *is* to do whatever out-of-title work your dispatchers are doing. By and large it is far easier in the long run to avoid this.

Besides examining what is and what is not part of the dispatcher's job, familiarization with expected duties also involves prioritizing the tasks. While answering the fire phone obviously takes precedence over recording alarms in the daily log, not all choices are that easy. What would you do when "the mayor is on line two" and "Ladder Six is out of service, so there's no truck company on the North Side"? Your answers depend on how many people you have working and what their powers and competencies are. There are many situations in the daily course of business that provoke discussions on priorities.

One of the ways to formalize the discussions so that your entire staff benefits from them is to provide available means for the working dispatchers to identify difficult situations as they occur. This gives them a way to share their concerns and to seek guidance from management. And it gives you a means to ensure more consistency and readiness in your operation. The easiest way to start the ball rolling is to make available a "problem sheet" (see Figure 6-1) on which the dispatcher can lay out his concerns. Introducing these sheets at your regular weekly training sessions opens up the discussion on the best ways for your department to respond to these situations. It also boosts morale by involving your staff in the problem-solving process.

Finally, when it comes to keeping tabs on expected duties in the larger departments, emergency communications managers should *do the job* for a full shift every quarter. They should answer fire phones, listen to the complaints from the public about open hydrants, too loud sirens, and swearing firefighters, juggle the radio calls, experience the off hours, and generally keep in touch with the job they are charged with managing. I know that there are managers who will groan that they don't have enough time as it is to run their shops effectively. The only warning I'll give you is, if you don't stay in contact with the basics, your shop will soon be running you!

KNOWLEDGE OF THE EQUIPMENT

You might think it goes without saying that your dispatchers should be capable of operating all the equipment in the communications center, yet I have seen many cases in which dispatch personnel have been unable to operate certain equipment. Some simply never received the necessary training. Others were scared of new equipment, something that often happens when computers are introduced into the operation. Still others developed attitude problems about certain parts of the operation. Some dispatchers will feel that certain duties are "beneath" them, and they simply won't bother to learn how to do them, or they'll tell a new guy that "It's been so long since I've done circuit testing that I'm just not sure that I'd be accurate." Of course, this couldn't happen without lazy managers as accomplices. The

Figure 6-1
DAILY PROBLEM SHEET

What is not working well?

_____

_____

_____

_____

_____

_____

_____

_____

_____

_____

_____

_____

_____

_____

_____

_____

Thanks for bringing this to our attention. We'll discuss it at our next weekly training meeting.

bottom line is that it's not unusual for there to be dispatchers who can't perform every function in the communications center. From your managerial point of view, while there will always be differences in talent, dedication, and "feel" for the job, you want all of these folks interchangeable in terms of their basic skills.

Skill checkoff sheets (see Figure 6-2), administered twice yearly on all operating equipment and on new equipment as it is acquired, will help maintain the competency of all staff. They should not induce a pressure-packed atmosphere but rather provide an opportunity for individuals to show what they can do. These forms obviously have use in quality-assurance activities for your training operation. One of the items you may wish to monitor for QA is whether or not lower-than-average competency in certain skills is subsequently made the topic of some remedial training.

If you are in any way involved in a merit pay system, you may wish to consider demonstration of basic competency on skill checkoffs as a requirement for consideration of salary increases.

An area that is frequently ignored in emergency communications is that of the field equipment and its applications. Many emergency communications managers just assume that their dispatchers know what tools the rescue truck carries and how they can be used. Many managers themselves don't have a real good idea of all that is out there. And yes, many dispatchers invest their own time in learning exactly what is available within their departments—but you can't assume that all your dispatchers will do so. Furthermore, if you rely on the informal method of "field training," then there is no rational justification for disciplining a dispatcher who fails to learn that which you made no formal effort to teach him.

It's a good idea to require that your dispatchers spend a tour with each type of company in your department. (You may want to check first with department lawyers regarding liability in the event of injury.) The field experience will contribute to his sense of urgency and motivation in certain situations. One of the frus-

Figure 6-2
TWICE YEARLY SKILL CHECK-OFF SHEET

Skill	Rating		
	1	2	3
Alarm Entry (CAD)			
Generator Check			
Circuit Testing			
Back-up Radio			
Status Board			
Log Entries			
Tape Recorders			
Notifications			
Security Check			
Safety Check			
First Aid			
Permits			
Specialty Tools			
Unit Locations			
Radio Procedure			
Courtesy			
Haz-Mat Resources			

Key: 1 = Excellent, 2 = Competent, 3 = Needs Improvement

trations of dispatching is that the dispatcher is distant from what he is delivering. Field experience will also serve to give him a positive feeling about his job by connecting him to the end product of his labor.

KNOWLEDGE OF THE TECHNIQUES

Aside from your ten-codes and the "First Commandment of Communications" ("Remain calm, dammit!"), there are many techniques you will want to impart to your dispatchers. Some of these are unique to your operation (for instance, what to do when atmospheric conditions enable another jurisdiction a hundred miles away to knock you off the air with their transmissions). Some require repeated training to master (such as how to respond dispassionately to a caller who verbally attacks you personally). A useful training method for many techniques is simulation. These can be taped or written, but are most effective when they most closely resemble actual operating conditions.

If it is possible to set up a training area where you can have simulated radio and telephone communications, do so. Then use the simulation experience to re-create every nerve-wracking communications experience you can think of. Have several field units call dispatch simultaneously, so that they garble almost all of each other's messages. The only word you can hear clearly is "Urgent!" Have the dispatcher direct, "All units stand by. Unit with the urgent message to ahead," and have two units garble one another again! See what your folks will do when faced with competing urgent messages. How are they going to prioritize them? At the same time, keep the phones ringing around them and people in the operations room yelling at them ("Anything back on that South Street box yet? I'm getting a lot of action on a building about three blocks over!" and "Hey, do you know that Ladder 114 is running with a spare rig today? It's a rear-mount, not a tower!" and "Is Engine 164 available from that brushfire yet?").

If you can, base your training exercises on actual events. Have the chief in charge at a third-alarm fire order a fifth alarm by radio. See if your dispatcher will verify that this request is for two additional alarms. See if your folks decide to transmit the fourth and fifth alarms simultaneously or if they wait a few minutes between each. The correct technique, again, depends on your jurisdiction. In rural and suburban areas where the responding units are geographically spread out, there is no need to wait between alarms, particularly if all the alarm assignments are preset. If you are in an urban setting where firehouses are often relatively close together, there is sometimes a benefit to waiting between the two alarms because the running times for the units on both alarms are pretty close to even in some cases. The last engine assigned on the fourth alarm may be expected to arrive at the scene at around the same time as the first two engines on the fifth alarm, for example. Waiting even a minute between alarms can help to ensure orderly arrival at the fire scene. This, in turn, helps in timely and useful placement of apparatus. It also decreases the likelihood of an apparatus accident in which two responding units, each blocking the sound of the other with its own siren and horns, enter the same intersection from different directions in an unusual response pattern.

If your training program is crafted in such a way as to include proper amounts of simulations and "real" experience from field familiarization, your dispatchers will start to think automatically in such terms as "altered response patterns." Field experience is absolutely necessary if your communications operation is to be a dynamic link among field units as well as between citizens and emergency assistance. Otherwise, there will always be a tendency to regard the end product of dispatching work as being the scribbling of units on the communications center's running board or the placement of unit chips on a status board or the typing of unit identities onto a computer screen. While dispatchers, for the most part, do their work inside the communications center, their minds must always be outside in the community they serve.

Make sure that your simulations include all facets of the

dispatcher's job. Have your people field calls from nosey reporters, from insurance adjusters working on commission who pretend to be reporters or officials, from the American Red Cross. And allow perhaps the most important opportunity to learn from simulations: Let your dispatcher *make mistakes!* Allow the errors to be carried through to the end. Let them see what happens if they inadvertently let "classified" information about a suspicious fire slip out to a reporter. When they see the ultimate outcome, it decreases the likelihood that they will ever jeopardize the prosecution of a real arsonist.

KNOWLEDGE OF THE PROCEDURES

It is relatively easy to assess competency in this area with written exams. Procedures are procedures, period. You have to know what they are. You have to know when to use them. In order to acquire that knowledge, your dispatchers have to spend time in the books. Have them begin with the operations manual.

What do you do if you have a fire in a U.S. Postal Service mailbox? . . . a Federal Express mailbox? . . . a manhole? . . . a traffic signal control box?. . . a power substation?. . .the airport? . . . aboard a ship?

Suppose there's a tank truck overturned on the interstate and it's leaking gasoline into the river. . .the hospital's power fails and its old generator isn't equal to the task of running its new equipment. . . there's a defective heating system in a school and 200 kids are showing signs of carbon monoxide poisoning.

Who gets notified? In what order? Why? Who handles the press? In multiagency operations, who's in charge?

Developing fluency with operating procedures is a grind, but it's a necessary one. Your training program must include drills to reinforce this data so that it kicks in as a reflex when you need it in a hurry. There's no magic way to do this. You simply have to work at it. The work is a little easier if your personnel spend time on the next area.

KNOWLEDGE OF THE JURISDICTION

One of the most annoying things I've seen in a communications center is when a dispatcher takes a call for an alarm at a supposed "intersection" of parallel streets! Besides studying operations manuals, dispatchers should spend time poring over maps. They'll be faced with times when the normal alarm assignment is not available and they're going to have to make decisions about who's next closest. They had better know the streets. I've seen dispatchers who could tell you from the house number— before the days of computer-assisted dispatch—what the cross streets were. And I've seen brand new dispatchers go out and buy themselves a map of their area so they could mark it up with notes to themselves about where firehouses were located, streets with similar names, and other tips that would eventually help them become professional in their work.

Good dispatchers pride themselves on knowing not only the streets and roads in their protection areas, but also what's on them. This provides a subconscious kind of help when making dispatch decisions. I remember getting a phone alarm for a small plane down in the middle of Brooklyn at two o'clock on a sunny summer afternoon. Now, there are special considerations for a plane down: Is it a cargo or passenger aircraft? How many passengers are on board and what kind of cargo is it carrying? What kind of fuel is it using? You would probably want to send the rescue company with its special tools and expertise, and notify the deputy chief, the press relations office, police, ambulances, FAA, and skatey-eight other people. However, I did none of these things.

The intersection at which this "crash" was reported had highrise apartments on two corners. There was a playground a block away, and retail stores on both streets. In other words, there would have been plenty of people around to see and *report* a plane crash. But I had only one telephone call and no pulled street boxes. We sent a first-alarm assignment, but, as suspected, the call was a hoax. Knowing what was on that corner, taken in consideration with the weather and the time of day, kept me from starting a lot of unnecessary work.

I've seen good dispatchers spend time quizzing each other on street and building locations—a kind of Trivial Pursuit of their protection area. Some of the best arguments I've seen in a dispatch center were over street locations and first-due assignments. But in addition to knowing the streets and the buildings in your protection area, all dispatchers must be aware of the special needs that are not always as obvious. The special protection problems posed by conditions not readily apparent to the untrained eye should be the focus of many training activities. These include such hidden concerns such as underground gas and oil pipelines, sewer systems, and utility tunnels. Other areas are not necessarily hidden but pose formidable potential protection and communications problems. For example, the average citizen looking across a harbor at a pretty island, connected to the mainland by a bridge, will see a tranquil picture. The dispatcher "looking for trouble" will wonder about how to get help to that island if a tanker collision in the harbor causes flames to scorch and perhaps structurally weaken the bridge.

Subways are a favorite topic for large-city field forces drills. They should also be a concern for communications personnel. Your technical support people should be looking at signal problems underground. Your dispatchers need maps of the system, including the spurs that aren't known to the public and the location of emergency exit manholes. Reports of smoke from manholes at multiple locations begin to make sense if they can be plotted along the route of underground tracks. A precise means of obtaining assurance from the trainmaster that power is off is a communications concern that is absolutely essential if field forces are to operate safely in subway systems or on or near surface tracks.

Harbor operations is another area that merits a lot of attention and planning. They frequently are sustained for long periods of time and require field command posts to control communications. Marine disasters also involve many other agencies, notably the U.S. Coast Guard, port officials, and officers and owners of the vessel(s) involved. Even international diplomacy can be a worry for field officers and communications personnel! You wouldn't want to suggest possible explanations for a collision since that may cast asperations on a specific vessel and, by association, the country of origin of either its crew or registry.

The ability to determine the cargo and number of crew members and passengers on a ship is vital in marine operations. The communications manager should establish channels of communication for data of this kind *before* any disaster occurs. Obtaining details on a ship's construction is also a skill your dispatchers need to know if you have a harbor in your protection area. Also very useful are establishing a connection with the towing lines/companies and knowing where burning ships are most likely to be towed.

The best way to anticipate Murphy's Law is for your personnel to brainstorm the jurisdiction's special needs. Seasonal concerns, haz-mat operations, brushfires and forest fires, and high life-hazard occupancies, such as schools, hospitals, theaters, and airports, need to be addressed. So do special operational concerns such as water supply and traffic control. A map overlay that pinpoints water sources in a given area is a very useful tool. If your dispatchers regularly interact with forest fire tower watchmen, it helps for each to have sense of what's going on at the other's end. For instance, making sure that the maps used for triangulation of smoke columns have the same designations in the dispatch center, on the rigs in the field, and in the tower will save a lot of response time during the windy and dry seasons each spring and fall.

ABILITY TO ASSESS THE WORKING ENVIRONMENT

In Chapter One we looked at the physical plant in which your dispatching operation is housed. Even if you've spent hundreds of hours planning your communications center, it takes some time actually running it to determine if those plans have translated well to practice. Your dispatchers need to know that there is some way in which they can call to your attention any necessary plant modifications. These changes may be needed to keep pace with changing technology or because increased demand for service has resulted in the hiring of more people who now need more space for lockers, parking, and eating as well as work space.

A good way to conduct a periodic, structured evaluation of the physical plant is to include it as part of your routine safety inspections. Remember that the time spent in prevention will be far less than that spent in intervention. It is far easier to solicit the input of your working staff than to have to deal with grievances over insufficient heating, inadequate toilet facilities, or whatever is bothering your troops. But if you ask people for their opinion, please remember two things:

1. Be prepared to hear ideas that may not be in agreement with yours!

2. *Do something* about the ideas whenever you can. If you have no intention to put some of the troop's suggestions to work, then don't bother trying to "stroke" them. They rightfully will be insulted and you will not get any further suggestions from them. Indeed, you will probably be ensuring decreased compliance with a lot of your directives!

If you spend a number of your training sessions on developing in each dispatcher the critical eye necessary to see if your plant safely serves your mission, it will be training time well spent.

AWARENESS OF STRESS

Sure, we're all aware that having a time-pressured, noisy, life-and-death situation thrust upon us without warning may cause our pulses to race a bit. We know that people screaming into the phone at us can cause a headache or two. There's no doubt that rotating shifts screw up our diets, our heads, and our social lives. But there's more to dispatcher stress than just the obvious. If you're going to formulate a healthy way to respond to job stress, then you're going to have to make sure you are aware of all of its sources.

Being "cool" under fire is not an easy task. Yet those who regularly listen to scanners frequently will comment that the dispatchers they hear are "unruffled," "detached," or even "unfeeling." It is usually a point of professional pride that a busy radio operator can control his emotions as well as the flow of traffic on his frequency. However, ulcers, migraine headaches, substance abuse, nocturnal grinding of teeth, dreaming about the job, and other stress-related disorders are common among dispatchers. There is no doubt that emergency communications personnel often pay the price for their outer "coolness."

The risk of stress disorder is high for the dispatcher. Ironically, the very internalization of stress puts the dispatcher at greater risk than if he displayed some symptoms of being worn down by the job. Unfortunately, many managers get promoted "away from" the job they are supposed to be managing and are as poorly equipped to recognize stress among their personnel as the average buff listening to his scanner. As I have noted several times already, the job of emergency communications is a dynamic one, constantly changing as the needs of society evolve. The fact that a manager once performed exceptionally well at the line level does not mean that he knows how to do that job today. So be warned: It just might be a little harder for a dispatcher to be "cool" today than it was fifteen years ago!

The dispatcher is an "insider." He knows that things are simply *not* always as under control as they seem. He knows that he can make a mistake. He knows that his mistake can kill somebody. He knows that, even if he does everything absolutely correctly, there's always the possibility that politics will rear its ugly head and look for a scapegoat. He may have already had an unfortunate disciplinary experience that makes him reluctant even to pick up the phone—the very essence of his job.

I knew a dispatcher who used to share, only half-kiddingly, this nightmare about having his performance reviewed by an investigation committee:

"I'm sitting in this hearing room and this old guy—who looks like the last fire he went to was started by Mrs. O'Leary's cow—is reading a decision to me. 'Dispatcher Roth, you realize now, of course, that after the plane crashed into the tank truck, causing its contents to leak into the basement of the hospital, you should have called the Center for Disease Control *before* you notified the Buildings Department and the FAA! This is obviously a serious infraction of the operating procedures of This Great Department, but since you've been such a good dispatcher for the past 16 years, we're inclined to go easy on you. So we're only going to take away three vacation days.' All for picking up the damn telephone!"

Naturally, this dispatcher was kidding, but there's a lot of truth said in jest. Make sure that you are not allowing political and disciplinary components of the job to add stress to the dispatchers' lives. Fear of failure is large enough because of the seriousness of the community consequences. Try and reduce job stress by allowing errors to be learning opportunities.

What are some other sources of stress that are not readily apparent? How about the idea that a dispatcher is, by definition, remote from his work? The fellow who takes a desperate screaming phone call from a mother trapped with her baby above the fire will tell you that there is no more helpless feeling in the world than waiting to find out if the field forces were proficient enough, timely enough, and lucky enough so that he was not the recipient of the last phone call of her life. How about ordered overtime as a big source of stress? It doesn't make any difference if no one turns a wheel all shift. The extra hours put in were not planned for and the dispatchers are taken away from nonwork (read that: "possibly relaxing") activities. How about never talking about stress, not even acknowledging its existence, as a source of stress in itself? Some of your dispatchers may be thinking, Well, it doesn't seem to bother anybody else. Maybe there's something wrong with me! And let's not forget all the external stressors that are in everybody's lives. The psychic energy that fuels a dispatcher's ability to deal with them can be exhausted by his job, and vice-versa. Dealing with holidays, losses, moving, loans, parenting, marital and relationship issues, and all the other life stressors can become much more difficult if you have a job that is eroding your coping skills as well.

How can you respond to this? Your training program can include role-playing situations in which your veteran dispatchers assume the part of the irritating caller. This serves the dual purpose of preparing the rookie for what is to come and allowing the senior people to give vent to their negative experiences in a way that is not seen as revealing a "weakness." Your dispatcher center can have a break room for down time away from the operating area. You can make sure your folks receive adequate compensation so that they don't have to seek overtime or a second job simply to support their families. You can make sure that you have enough people to meet the demand. Doing the work of two or more people on a consistent basis is an express ticket to burnout. You can mandate a maximum interval between vacations, making sure that each dispatcher gets away from work sometime during the year. You devote one of each quarter's weekly training sessions solely to stress management, teaching relaxation and recognition techniques. You can organize, enroll in, or recommend an employee assistance program that will enable your personnel to get some help in dealing with life stressors when needed. You can spend some time analyzing the outcomes of nonproductive responses to stress. This kind of study often enables the individual to focus on the big picture and avoid anger, drinking, and other self-defeating behaviors.

It should be obvious by now that stress is related to all the other aspects of training. By taking time to build a training program that truly equips your dispatchers to do their jobs, you will be avoiding the most stressful situation of leaving them on their own in an emergency. Without the resources, procedures, equipment, support, or knowledge to meet the demands placed on them, they will feel "left hanging in the breeze." A job that engenders that kind of feeling is not one for which you want to get up every morning!

Stress reduction for both you and the people you supervise is also related to just about everything else in this book. Failure to address properly the issues surrounding the working environment, the day-to-day operation of the job, and respect for the individual will ensure all involved a great deal of avoidable stress. The fact that you are even reading this book, however, suggests that you are well on your way to preempting that situation.

CHAPTER SEVEN

Computers In Dispatching

S TAYING ON TOP OF a constantly changing galaxy of protection responsibilities is a major challenge for fire service leaders. Many have chosen to meet that challenge in part by making use of available modern technology. One technological tool that may be considered by the emergency communications manager is computer-assisted dispatching (CAD). Computer-assisted dispatching, while a long-time fact of fire service life in many locales, remains a rumor in other areas. For some of the larger departments with the budget to do so, planning for CAD started 20 years ago. For others, their current task is just getting a handle on what CAD might mean for their departments. Some departments use computers in and around their emergency communications operations but really could not be considered to be running CAD systems. Others don't have the assessment expertise to define an efficient application of computer technology for themselves. Still others have taken a very well-educated look at what's available and what it costs and have been very comfortable with the decision that CAD is not for them.

How do you define and apply CAD for your operation? Although there is always a competitive pressure to have the latest "toys" when it comes to CAD, the basic, responsible question you have to ask is, What more can computers do for us—with more speed, accuracy, and cost efficiency—than we are currently doing manually?

ANTICIPATED CONCERNS

Let's start by taking a look at what traditionally have been the anticipated concerns of departments looking into CAD systems. Then we'll look at some of the unanticipated concerns that actually have developed.

Does this mean I'm out of a job? For the individual dispatcher, the primary concern is the basic one of survival. Visions of "being replaced by a computer" haunt many a dispatcher when the early CAD rumors start to float into the emergency communications center. This fear seems to originate from the misconception that the cost savings associated with computerization come solely from eliminating those expensive components of the system: people. Nothing could be further from the truth. In many cases, depending on the volume of traffic handled, change to a CAD system actually increased the number of dispatchers needed to process alarms.

The reason for this lies in the nature of the relationship between the computer and the dispatcher. No matter how fast the computer may be or how large its data capacity, there remains a bottleneck at the point of information transfer from the dispatcher to the CAD system. Data must be input at a keyboard, and a CAD system handles only one task at a time at each work station. While different facets of the fire alarm system (reading signals from street boxes and mobile data transmission systems used to update units' status, for example) can be monitored and processed to a point by a CAD system without dispatcher oversight, the critical aspects of fire alarm dispatching—quickly and accurately receiving and interpreting data from callers and deciding how to respond to an incident—present themselves *one at a time* to a dispatcher.

Humans, especially those who work in busy emergency dispatching centers, far surpass computers when it comes to communicating on several levels at the same time. In a manual dispatching system, a single dispatcher may be wearing half a headset, cradling a phone to the other ear while listening to the radio, watching the alarm lights and blinking incoming fire phone lines, moving unit chips or magnets on a status board or writing notes on a running board, making hand signals to the radio dispatcher regarding which "on the air" units to assign to an active alarm, counting the taps of incoming signals and relating them instantly to the outstanding active alarms, handing alarm assignment cards to a bell transmitter operator or a voice alarm operator, and wondering what's for supper!

In the best of the CAD systems, each of these functions takes place separately, and where decisions are to be made—the *human* factor—the choices are presented to the dispatchers as a series of separate *single* events. The computer can do an excellent job of receiving and storing data. In a manual system you might worry about missing a box alarm that comes in on a circuit in which the buzzer has gone on the bum. The computer will always catch that alarm. But in the computerized system, entering unit status or data from a telephone alarm and picking up on-the-air units are separate, discrete functions. And supper doesn't get addressed at all!

Planners have conducted long and tedious time-and-motion studies in trying to get some idea of what response time minimums to build into requests for bids from CAD hardware and software vendors. After all, there's no sense in spending money on a fire alarm dispatching system that's going to be slower than the one it's replacing. A man with a stopwatch and a clipboard would wait for a fire alarm—either telephone or pulled box—to come into the communications center. The times from receipt to dispatch and receipt to arrival were measured in the manual system. These were the elapsed times that a prospective CAD system would have to match or beat in order to be considered for purchase. It became apparent rather quickly that, for an individual alarm, no computer could match the proficiency of a good dispatcher.

Let's examine how an alarm for a structure fire in Brooklyn is handled under the CAD system and compare it to the "old" manual system:

In the CAD system, a ringing "fire phone" is answered by an alarm receipt dispatcher (ARD) who sits in front of a telephone console and a CRT. From this position he can answer either telephone alarms or alarms originating at voice-operated fire alarm boxes on street corners and in some buildings. As the ARD answers the call, he calls up an alarm screen on his CRT by hitting a button on a keyboard. The alarm screen has a variety of empty "fields" into which the dispatcher types in data received from the caller. Typing in an address will automatically give a box number and cross streets. The dispatcher enters a letter code that indicates the type of fire reported. The computer is prompted to assign certain equipment to specific letter codes. A fire reported in a school or hospital, for example, would cause the computer to recommend a response of more companies than a vacant structure. A nonstructural code would result in the computer recommending only one engine. Before releasing his alarm screen to the next step in the processing of the alarm, the ARD also keys in a call-back number, if he can get one, and other pertinent information such as a floor and apartment number. By hitting a release button his keyboard, the ARD sends the alarm to the decision dispatcher (DD). The DD gets an audible prompt and a light on his console that tells him he has a message waiting. If he has nothing else working at the moment, hitting a "next" button will bring him that alarm immediately. If he has several other alarms coming in at the same time, they will queue up at the DD workstation—that is, they line up in the computer awaiting action. Theoretically, the computer can queue alarms according to receipt time (first come, first served) or according to coded severity (structure fires before car fires). In the Brooklyn system (part of FDNY's *Starfire* CAD network), however, alarms line up in order of receipt. The DD can pull a more urgent alarm out of the queue sequence (if he is aware of the relative urgency) by displaying the queue on his screen and commanding that it be processed first.

The DD gets a recommended dispatch screen that shows him the reported alarm, along with the alarm assignment for that location and the status of the units on that assignment. If he agrees with the computer's recommendation, he hits "Release" and the alarm is on its way to a variety of places.

If all of the recommended units to be dispatched are available in quarters, the alarm prints out on teleprinters in each affected fire station. The housewatchman acknowledges receipt of the alarm by hitting a button at the teleprinter station. If some of the units are on the air, the alarm is immediately flashed to the screen in front of the radio dispatcher, who calls for those units to respond. If a unit is in quarters but its teleprinter is down, or if an acknowledgement is not received in 30 seconds, the alarm also flashes to a screen in front of the voice alarm dispatcher, who contacts the units verbally over the firehouse PA systems. When the first-arriving unit pulls up at the scene, the officer lets the radio dispatcher know, and a code is punched into the computer that logs the arrival time.

A dispatcher under the manual system, doing several things at once, can often "beat" the CAD dispatch time. If, for example, the ringing fire phone was picked up by a dispatcher who was aware of a current "on-the-air" status of a unit assigned to the alarm being reported, it would not be unusual for him to gesture in the direction of the radio dispatcher while he was still in the process of recording the data. Or a radio dispatcher might over-hear the receipt of a telephone alarm because the ARD taking the call might purposely raise his voice a little. Having heard a report of a building fire at Flatbush and Atlantic avenues, and knowing that the first-due truck, Ladder 105, is available on the air from a false alarm on the other side of their district, the radio man is pressing his transmit key and calling the truck even before the ARD has gotten a call-back number, a floor or apartment number, and a box number. Before the ARD is even off the phone, the first-due truck is rolling to the alarm—usually with a sketchy preliminary report like "Start out for Flatbush and Atlantic, report of a building fire, particulars to follow"—in less than 10 seconds from the time the phone rang. The *Starfire* system averages 40 seconds from the first citizen contact until the time the alarm reaches the housewatch desk.

In a manual system, with knowledgeable dispatchers, speed can be enhanced for individual alarms without accuracy being sacrificed. Of course, if there is a heavy volume of fire traffic, CAD does better with average response times. The manual system picks up time over the CAD system because:

1. The ARD in a manual system does not have to have all the information before causing companies to roll. Because he wants to have all the pertinent data print out on the fire ticket at the housewatch, the ARD in a CAD system must take the time to make sure that floor, apartment, and phone numbers are printed in the appropriate fields on the alarm screen before he can release that alarm to the DD responsible for getting the companies rolling.

2. In a manual system, the ARD can signal relative urgency of alarms by standing up, raising his voice, waving his arms, or (as I've seen happen more than once) throwing something in the direction of the man running the status board. The dispatcher who assigns companies from a response card is able to bypass alarms received before the more urgent building fire by simply putting that assignment card on the top of his pile. In the CAD system, the DD first must be aware that the more urgent alarm exists. Even if the ARD were to signal that fact, there is little that can be done outside of the system that generates the incidents. The DD would still have to wait until the ARD finished data input and released the alarm to the DD before the alarm could be

transmitted to any units on the air or in quarters. If that alarm is not the next in time sequence, the DD must execute two more maneuvers to get to the urgent alarm.

In a CAD system, absolutely everything a dispatcher does is quantified. A car fire across the street from an apartment house can easily generate a dozen calls. In the manual system, these calls would result in the generation of a single fire ticket to dispatch an engine to the fire. The other eleven tickets would wind up in the trash basket. In fact, a dispatcher in a manual system often will simply yell across the room, "Hey, Henry! You got a car at Clinton and Congress?" If the answer is yes, the dispatcher who just took the most recent call will relax, knowing that the incident is covered.

In a CAD system, alarm receipt dispatchers simply enter alarm data into the system. "Potential duplicate" alarms are suggested to the DD for his action. If he decides that the potential duplicate is a separate event, he can dispatch another assignment to it. If he considers it to be another call for an alarm already covered, he can close the subsequent alarm as a duplicate. The big difference, though, in the CAD system is that either way—duplicate or not—the alarm gets recorded. It figures in the computer-generated statistics at the end of the day for alarms processed. It also figures, in real time, into the calculation of the alarm rate per hour. The old system did not give dispatchers credit for all the work they did. CAD statistics regarding alarms processed, which were essentially unobtainable in the manual system (except in "guestimate" form, as in the workload multiplier described in Chapter Five), make a very strong case for dispatcher job security!

Can CAD do the job? A Philadelphia dispatcher expressed this thought some years ago: "It's nice, I suppose, that a CAD system will generate all kinds of reports and statistics. But will it get the right fire engines to the right places at the right times?" In other words, can CAD do the job—accurately, safely, and quickly? Most of the big departments that have been using CAD for years provide the answer to this concern. The answer is yes . . . but you have to be prepared to spend some bucks! The FDNY *Starfire* system cost more than $15 million in its first ten years. It has shortened response times and provides a great deal of statistical data called management information. But not everybody has that kind of money or has the need to generate reports. Not everyone is unhappy with their response times; unless you have a *substantial* alarm volume, your response times will be as quick, if not quicker, if you have knowledgeable, efficient dispatchers. And not everybody has had a positive experience with CAD the first time around.

It is possible for you to invest in smaller personal or business computers to support your operations. In a survey of fire departments in North America by *Fire Engineering* magazine, 94 percent of respondents indicated that they used computers in their departments. These departments were pretty much evenly divided among paid, volunteer, and combination; they ranged in size from 15 to 1,400 members and covered the full range of protection responsibilities from urban areas to vast expanses of desert. Very few of the almost 100 respondents, though, used computers in the generation of incident response. Reported use covered a broad range of applications: equipment location, hydrant test records, payroll, purchasing, prefire plans, hose test records, census, haz-mat information (listed both generically and according to specific address or box locations), personnel lists, duty roster, EMS reports, inventory control, word processing, extraordinary medical hazards (persons on respirators or using tanked oxygen in private residences), and fund raising.

Several departments report using various "part-way" CAD operations in which dispatchers have computerized assistance in certain components of the dispatch process. Such assistance might include receiving cross streets and a box number for any address entered, or the ability to monitor unit status; the dispatchers might be able to look up landmarks, floor plans, or specific alarm assignments to augment the manual generation of an alarm. These are not true CAD systems, but they do assist dispatchers in their work. And, for the most part, the compromise is an acceptable one. The reason for compromise is not that technology isn't available to computerize any dispatch operation; the thing that's usually not available is cash!

Loss of tradition. A third fear expressed by potential CAD users is the loss of tradition. This fear turned out to be the one most often realized. There is no doubt that installation of CAD changes much of the "romance of the airwaves." There are new terms (ARD, DD, CRT) introduced to the dispatching vocabulary. In many cases, the bells that used to clang out the response signals are gone, replaced by the quiet whirring of dot matrix printers. Long-time scanner listeners lament the digital radio transmission of unit status. The verbal messages, after all, were far more entertaining. Gone, too, in many CAD operations is the background noise by which radio listeners—buffs and firefighters alike—used to tell that something big was breaking, even before the alarm was transmitted. The bells, the shouting, and the ringing phones—and even the threat to occupational health of the dispatchers who were exposed to this cacophony day after day— are now sometimes spoken of in the terms of hushed reverence reserved for "the good old days."

I have several responses to this concern. One is that, steeped in tradition as the fire service is, the primary mission—saving lives and protecting property—has never changed. If computers enhance your department's capability to achieve this mission, then utilizing CAD will be very much in keeping with that tradition. As to the many folks who will miss "the romance of the airwaves," I say, first, they either have short memories or no appreciation of the history of fire communications. It was not all that long ago that there were no radio transmissions. Telegraph signals, gongs, and even messengers on horseback or bicycle were the means by which help was summoned. Secondly, although it certainly can be exciting to listen to the fire radio, we are not in the entertainment business. If there is a better way of doing our jobs, then we should do it! It is up to you to decide if CAD is "a better way" for your department. To further help you make that decision, we'll take a look now at some of the unanticipated CAD problems that have actually surfaced after systems were operating.

UNANTICIPATED PROBLEMS

We will not use this space to examine technical bugs in your software or glitches in your hardware. For one thing, these are hardly unanticipated. For another, they are the types of problems that are usually very specific to your operation, and your technical support people will weed them out as they crop up. What is relevant to our discussion are some general problems that were experienced in more than one CAD operation and a few of the responses to counter them.

The physical and psychological effects to the operators of CAD equipment proved to be a major concern. Newspaper writers and airline reservation clerks, among others, have long been aware of the physiological consequences of sitting in front of a CRT all day. Glare off the screen can cause headache and eyestrain. This was resolved by changing the configuration and type of the interior lighting, adding glare shields to the screens, altering window treatments to regulate light entrance, or repositioning workstations so that natural light from windows was not interfering with CRT visibility. Glare also can directly impede the processing of alarms: It's hard to enter data into an alarm screen field if you're not sure where the cursor is! You'll want to make sure that the problem is solved before you go on line.

More complex visual impairments have been reported by dispatchers who have been concentrating on CRTs for hours. These screens, like your television, flicker imperceptibly but constantly. Some dispatchers reported that they had difficulty driving home at night, complaining of decreased visual acuity in darkness and a very slow light-to-dark adaptation time. For some, this meant that they were virtually blind after a car passing in the other direction momentarily flashed across their field of vision. One dispatcher got a note from his opthamologist suggesting that he "stay away from CRTs for a few days." He began to feel and function better, but his bosses were faced with the problem of what to do with a dispatcher who, for the time being at least, was medically barred from operating their new million-dollar system. Making sure that personnel have some time away from the screen each shift seems to be the answer to "CRT strain."

Other physical complaints were familiar to secretaries but not to dispatchers. For years, typing teachers have warned their students that improperly placed keyboards and chairs cause muscle strain in the neck, lower back, and upper body. Add CRTs to the list of things that, when put in the wrong place, can literally be a pain in the neck! In many of the "old," manual dispatching systems, the job was often done standing up. That's virtually impossible with a CRT, so pay attention to the quality of your chairs. Make sure they're adjustable, with good lumbar support. Don't be afraid to ask the local typing teacher to come in and explain foot, arm, and chair placement.

In addition to physical complaints, there were a host of unforeseen psychological factors in daily CAD operations that had to be addressed. These ranged from the increased sense of fatigue experienced when dispatchers had their workload systematically quantified ("I knew we were busy, but I didn't realize we were *this* busy!" said one Brooklyn dispatcher, looking at a summary CRT screen that showed his borough was currently processing 144 alarms an hour) to a sense of being left out of the big picture. "This system breaks everything down into smaller parts," said one dispatcher who had been working a CAD operation for three years. "The other night I was working as an alarm receipt dispatcher and it was busy: brushfires, dumpsters, open hydrant complaints—the regular summer rush. Then I got a call from a radio station asking about a fire in a hospital that they had heard on their scanner. I felt like a jerk, since they knew more about it than I did. I was busy in my own little electronic corner of the world. In the old days, this never would have happened." He was right, of course. In the old days, everybody knew everything that was going on, whether they needed to or not. The question is, though, is it *better* for everybody to have that constant deluge of data washing over them?

On the other side of the coin is what happens after dispatchers become acclimated to CAD and it is taken away from them. That's right, despite a lot of cynicism and dispatcher resistance to CAD at the outset, it quickly becomes a case of, How did we ever do it for so long without CAD? In fact, a good CAD system tends to spoil dispatchers—so much so that on days when it was known in advance that the CAD system would be down for scheduled maintenance and system updates, FDNY would experience an increase in dispatcher sick leave. This was not an isolated phenomenon. Sergeant Gary Mann of the Montgomery County Emergency Operations Center in Rockville, Maryland says, "When the system goes down, it's difficult. Not just for the new employees, but also for those of us with 20 years of experience. You get used to the easy way." Russell D. Ramsey, former chief dispatcher in charge of Brooklyn operations, takes it a step further: Getting used to the easy way is "not so much the problem, of course, as is forgetting how to do it the harder way!" Many localities, realizing the potential for losing "manual fluency" in their dispatch operations, routinely take their CAD system down whether or not system maintenance is needed. Says Captain Robert Guzzi, communications officer for the Oakland, California Fire Department, "If you don't use it, you lose it." He reports that his dispatcher training includes a lot of manual operations. "You never know when you're going to have to switch. We want everybody to be able to function in either mode."

Just as the pocket calculator has made it impossible for many folks to balance their checkbooks without it, so can a good CAD system lull its operators into becoming dangerously dependent on it. The possibility that dispatchers' manual communications skills will atrophy from underuse is real. Ironically, the better your system, the more likely is such loss of manual skills. FDNY's *Starfire* has 98.3 percent system reliability. Of the 1.7 percent down time in a year, 1.1 percent is planned. This leaves only 0.6 percent unplanned down time. Chief Dispatcher Mike Vitucci of the CAD Operations Unit says, "It's a great system. However, when you run at that level of reliability with CAD, you naturally tend to become sloppy manually."

Most dispatchers will not argue against the necessity for systems redundancy. "Better safe than sorry" is the generally accepted philosophy here. It is imperative to view your manual system as the backup for the CAD system. There is, though, a large hitch to bringing your system down purposely to ensure manual fluency: the possibility of increased response times directly attributable to the use of the manual dispatching mode. The thinking goes that a "flurry" of alarms processed under the manual system may result in a later-arriving first-alarm assignment for *some* alarm in that flurry. If a substantial fire loss occurs, a litigant could possibly argue that the city was not using every means at its disposal to effect the fastest response to a fire. Therefore, should you have a CAD operation and plan to take down your system for routine manual operations—a need that is well recognized throughout the computerized operations in the fire service—it is important that you first obtain an educated opinion from legal counsel regarding potential liability. If you decide that you cannot take your system down, make other provisions for manual training. Use a mock-up operations area if you have to, but make sure that those manual skills do not waste away and leave you with no backup to your CAD system.

The possible uses of computers are limited only by your

budget and your imagination. You can have the computer turn on the lights and open the firehouse doors when it transmits an alarm. Your fire investigation folks can run fire reports against building permits to see if, for example, a certain contractor's work seems to be experiencing a greater-than-expected alarm incidence (giving rise to such questions as, Was this contractor using substandard wiring? and Who was the building inspector on these jobs?).

Tons of data can be stored—water supply, prefire plans, you name it. You can have that data available by dispatcher request or via system-generated prompts (a box is pulled, comes up on a CRT, and the message blinks at the dispatcher: There is a preplan on file for an occupancy at this box location). A popular capability in *Starfire* is to call up a map on the CRT screen that will display the geographical location of any box number you pick, or, if you prefer, the locations of all the currently active alarms.

Now, to be sure, you don't need all these "buzzers and bells" to make a good CAD system, if you need a system at all. After all, as one respondent to the *Fire Engineering* survey put it, "A $50,000 computer replaces a 39-cent pen and a $50 file card cabinet *and* requires a lot of training!"

If you decide to computerize, ask your vendors for a list of all their customers. See what similar jurisdictions are doing. What works? What's their biggest gripe? Make sure that you have technical support available, either in-house or by way of a service contract. I've heard many more arguments against "canned" software than for it. It appears, from what the users are saying, that you do best with a system tailored to your needs. This costs more but apparently is better than spending less on a system that doesn't fit the bill. And make sure that you have somebody on staff who not only knows how to use the system but can also impart this information to the rest of your staff. All of this sounds a lot like planning, and that's the topic of our next chapter.

CHAPTER EIGHT

Planning

HAVING DONE EVERYTHING NECESSARY to keep your operation and the people who run it sharp, you now have the opportunity to sit back and let it hum along, right? Well, not exactly. To be sure, if all the elements covered in Chapters One through Seven—from plant selection to computer assistance—have been addressed and fine-tuned, then you shouldn't be limited to the management of crises. Things *should* hum along a little better. But that doesn't mean you'll have time to sit back and watch the gears turn. You have managerial responsibilities yet to meet.

Many management specialists recognize four "classic" functions of management: leadership, organization, control, and planning. If you have followed this book so far, you have, by exercising your leadership, established systems that will attend to the organization and control of your operation. Once this is done, you will have more of your working time available to devote to planning.

What is planning? In the spirit of simplicity, let's define planning as "getting ready"—that's all, just "getting ready."

"So I get ready, I've done my planning. Once I've gotten ready, that's it. Planning is finished, right?"

That's true only if you accept the notion that the fire service is static. In reality, one of the major challenges for fire service leaders is keeping pace with the constantly changing world they protect—so your planning is *never* finished. It is an ongoing exercise that reflects the dynamic nature of the service.

What's your plan for planning? All large tasks are more easily attacked when broken down into components. A list of your activity subheadings might include planning for physical plant, personnel, budget, operations, and training. Let's take a look at some of the concerns in each of these categories.

Physical plant. This includes both inside and outside plant concerns. If, after finishing Chapter One, you decide that your plant is not up to par, you'll want to list the changes needed for safe and efficient operation. Then you'll have to pare your "wish" list down to a "needs" list.

Prioritize your needs. Safety issues come first and fall into two categories:

1. Public safety. If anything about your physical plant works against the accurate and speedy receipt, interpretation, and transmission of data—your primary mission—then it is in the way of public safety.

2. Personal safety. If your physical plant is in such poor shape that working in it presents real hazards to the personnel assigned there, you have a compromise of personal safety. This, obviously, can also threaten public safety.

After safety concerns you'll need to examine two cyclic needs: preventive maintenance and capital replacement. Since capital replacement is so closely tied to fiscal planning, we'll look at it under the "budget" heading. Preventive maintenance, however, is a lot like fire prevention: It's a whole lot easier and cheaper to prevent than to intervene. Situations that call for intervention—such as finding out that the support stanchions on your primary transmission tower are structurally compromised by rust—generally occur in a crisis mode.

You can avoid the frantic response to crisis by the methodical, even plodding means of preventive maintenance schedules. You pick the way you want to be reminded of when to give things a coat of paint, a cleaning, a line test, or simply a good look. Pencil them into your day book for the year ahead, have them posted on your office wall, or establish a "tickler" file to jog your memory. Any of these is better than having a piece of plaster hit you in the head one day!

So much of the advice in this book calls for taking a global approach to managing all your operational components that by now you should be thinking of one system part in terms of the others. One of the best ways to determine the effectiveness of your preventive maintenance program is to combine maintenance and safety rounds each month. These rounds also provide an excellent opportunity for quality assurance studies of both your maintenance functions and your managerial performance. Machines will break down occasionally. That is why you have redundant systems such as a generator for power failures, a backup radio transmitter, and spare alarm boxes to replace those destroyed in auto accidents. However, when any component of your physical plant fails, be it the plumbing, the file cabinets, or the roof gutters, the questions that naturally follow are, Could this failure have been prevented? and Could it have been foreseen, and by whom?

Preventive maintenance is continuous planning. While it is not especially glamorous, it is both essential to emergency communications and appreciated by those who fall into the next category of planning:

Personnel. Our brief study of employment planning (Chapter Two) outlines some of the considerations for personnel: technological forecasts, economic forecasts, human resource supply and demand, retirement planning, recruitment, wage and salary competitiveness, and overtime. That list gives you a starting point from which to operate when selecting candidates. It's also useful in personnel planning, the basis of which lies in the long-term answer to the question, Will I have enough people to do the job? Remember that this is *long-term*. You're not just figuring out FTEs for the next year here. You need to study turnover rates, expected retirements and promotions, and negotiated contract changes (which can accelerate retirements, change working conditions in a way that people may want to or have to leave, or increase minimum staffing requirements). Also, make sure that you are tracking workload. Just because five folks handled it for the past decade, you can't sit back and assume that the status quo is sufficient. It may be. But you need to prove that to yourself every few years.

You can add another dimension to the personnel planning process by modifying your original question somewhat and asking yourself, Will I have enough *qualified* people to do the job? To answer this question you must consider job descriptions and technological forecasts. Will you require your dispatching personnel to use computer-assisted dispatch systems? Will they need to be able to do some troubleshooting in a CAD system? Will they have to have a passible degree of computer literacy so that they can describe their operational needs and concerns to the CAD support people? Will your dispatchers have to pass a minimum competency exam for typing? Is your system going to change so radically that you'll have to provide the means for veteran personnel to acquire newer skills? Are you going to need additional titles in your operation? Need a computer programmer? Service tech? How about a training officer, or a liaison officer to work with other city agencies? In a smaller operation, the emergency communications manager can perform training and liaison functions. In a larger communications division one person can't wear all those hats. The decision will be up to you, of course. But if you are at least routinely examining these areas, your decisions will not be made by default. You will have a handle on your personnel needs. When you have a good sense of that, you will have a key to the next area of planning:

Budget. Do you know the life expectancy of each piece of

capital equipment you use? Are you aware of the projected costs for the year of replacement? Will growth or change in occupancies in your area of protection require additional equipment? Is changing technology suggesting that you do not have sufficient equipment to meet demand for service in the fastest way possible? Do you need a microfiche system? A computer? Will the local lawmakers accept your proposal that new occupancies share in the cost for new cable installations, alarm boxes, or repeater stations? Will a chemical plant pay for the cost of a dedicated phone line so they can have "hot line" access to dispatch? Are you able to share support personnel—and thus costs—with other departments?

With regard to your physical plant: Look to see if your planning activities reveal a need for capital construction. Ask yourself if preventive maintenance activities are sufficiently funded. You can begin to get a sense of this by reviewing several related aspects of your management operation such as your monthly maintenance/safety rounds. Are the same items cropping up again and again? Are the same safety concerns the repeated subjects of costly grievances by your workers? If you have some question as to whether or not your preventive maintenance function is effective, build a quality assurance study around it. Then step back and look at all the management information available to you.

For example, if repeated employee grievances over a three-year period suggest that your emergency communications center is simply too damned cold in the winter, take a look at why. If you find repeated small-parts breakdowns, analyze your HVAC preventive maintenance program. A QA study could analyze the number of hours spent in preventive maintenance versus the number of hours spent in processing grievances, hours lost to sick calls directly attributed to poor working conditions, and hours spent trying to find replacement personnel to cover those sick calls. For good measure, factor in the overtime pay and the cost of processing it. *Then* decide if your preventive maintenance function is sufficiently funded. (Like the man says, "You can pay me now or pay me later!") A quality assurance follow-up will make it clear whether or not your intervention made any difference. The follow-up might indicate adding a new category to your monthly rounds.

Again, notice how managerial concerns tie together and support one another. The safety/maintenance monthly rounds form is introduced in Chapter One, its regular review is advised in Chapter Five, and its value in planning is highlighted here in Chapter Eight. You can use any of these ideas singularly or as an integrated way of managing your emergency communications system. Assuming a lot of new concepts all at once can be somewhat overwhelming at first, but your ultimate goal—having a cohesive and smooth-running operation—makes it worth the effort. Having a global perspective will also help your pitch come budget time. A well-managed, efficient operation always translates into more bang for your buck, something your city or county fathers always like to point out at election time.

Along the lines of stretching your dollars is the question, Is there a cheaper yet equally effective way to do the same thing? This may involve something as seemingly simple as a telephone line audit. It's not unusual in midsize and large corporations to find current billing for lines removed years before; that may be the case with you. Or your billing plan may have been set up before the divestiture of Ma Bell. Volume- and time-specific rates may now be available to you. There are many cost-cutting avenues to explore: Is your lighting the most efficient it can be? Your heating and air conditioning? How about your emergency generator? Can you use lighter-grade computer paper? Can you "contract out" some support services? Can you do better with a municipal group purchase plan? How effective is your scheduling? We have already seen, in Chapter Three, how creative scheduling can reduce personnel costs. In fact, many of the points I've already made about personnel and work environment will help you decrease personnel costs associated with injuries, labor disputes, overtime, sick leave, and overall efficiency.

Remember, it's absolutely essential to keep intimately in touch with all aspects of the operation you supervise and to be responsive to all personnel. The last thing you need is to find yourself before the county budget committee facing questions to which you do not have the answers. Maintain contact with your superiors as well as your subordinates. A county commissioner or city councilperson is far less likely to blindside you on an issue if he's familiar with the problem and understands your position. If there is a problem, let him know directly or through one of his staff. But don't go outside the chain of command and don't make continual whining complaints. Make "courtesy calls." If you talk to a staff member, get his name and note the time. Use a recorded phone at all times. Keep a special file for notes you've made on the call if such calls aren't an expected part of your routine notifications and therefore aren't logged in your notifications book. Always present the information in terms of its practical use to the individual you are calling: "I know you're busy, but I figured you might be hearing from the local papers about the main transmitter having some significant down time for the past few hours. We have it adequately backed up with our emergency transmitter. The audio quality is not the same, but we have enough power to cover the county." After you've done that, get your own budget pitch in smoothly: "We'll look okay for having the redundancy in the system, but someday soon it might be a good idea to consider a new primary transmitter." You don't need to do anything but plant the seed at this point. Don't bother telling him that Marconi made the backup system or that you fear a conflagration will consume the town someday soon. He hears dollar-related predictions of doom from his constituencies all the time. What you *can* do, though, is follow up your courtesy call with a calm and reasoned letter outlining your assessment of the department's needs in the area. This, of course, will have to be routed through the chain of command. And I shouldn't have to tell you by now to keep a copy! The next link in the chain may decide not to forward your observations. If that's the case, rest assured you've done what you can. But keep the copy in case Murphy's Law strikes again.

It's not a happy thought, but if an avoidable tragedy should occur because of an official failure to respond to your documented concerns, you have to be prepared for the possibility of political repercussions. The higher-up who decided your concerns were without merit (or, even more distasteful to consider, decided they had merit but that their revelation would reflect negatively on his performance) might be looking for a scapegoat. That's where your record keeping comes in handy. Putting things in writing takes some time and effort, but you have to consider the cost of not doing it. In some cases, that price could be further advancement in your career. Always cover your flanks with your typewriter, word processor, or tape recorder.

A final budget consideration lies in the area of community relations. If your dispatchers are courteous in dealing with callers, if they get involved in local charitable causes such as walkathons and telethons (telethons are especially well-suited for dispatching personnel who are used to doing so much telephone work anyway. The pitch is, "We are always there when you need to call us *for* help. Now we're here because we need you to call us *with* help"), and if they have a generally positive image in the community, there will be at least some degree of positive predisposition toward your cause when it come to public budget discussions.

Operations. Planning in this area involves two basic categories:

1) Area of protection—You need to keep up on changes in your jurisdiction. One of the best ways to do this is to arrange for your department to be notified whenever a building permit is granted. A surprising number of jurisdictions don't have this kind of interagency communication built into their systems. Having it will keep you abreast of new developments, new streets, new occupancies, and a lot of changes in old occupancies. It is always

better to find out about these things before an incident commander calls you with some startling news—such as a report of
hazardous-materials warnings posted on the side of what until
recently had been a rather benign warehouse full of bales of rags!

An obvious way to keep posted on your area of protection is
to take a ride through it periodically. There is a developing school
of thought in the field—particularly among providers of contract
services who are looking to minimize costs and maximize prof-
its—that you can centralize communications for multiple jurisdictions in an operations area remote from those which are being
served. The proponents of this idea also believe that you can staff
such a communications center with dispatchers who are not
personally familiar with the areas from which the phone calls are
coming. It should be clear to anyone who has worked in more
than one jurisdiction that such a set-up can leave the dispatcher
without a crucial understanding of the caller's situation. The
dispatcher may have enough information to get by for the majority of your calls. But when unusual circumstances surround
either the caller (fire is reported by a visiting cousin from another
part of the country) or the area (a critical combination of to-
pography and weather conditions that may alter response patterns; very recent emergency road repairs; "moving day" in a
college town that clogs the streets around campus; radically
different traffic patterns around a church on a Sunday morning)
his familiarity with the district will make a significant difference
in response time. Not enough can be said for the value of a
dispatcher's working knowledge of his protection district.

Your dispatching staff should notice changes in the protection
district just by keeping their eyes open on the way to work. This
informal data gathering is by no means restricted to the communications personnel; firefighters, too, can become involved in
the effort on their trips to and from work and during their tours of
duty. It helps to have a "what's new" channel open by which you
all can communicate data on the changes in your protection area.
This can be a monthly polling of the companies, a periodic

brainstorming session between firefighters and dispatchers, or a less formal system of sending along "FYI" memos whenever appropriate. In some cases the first your troops may hear of a significant change is by reading the local newspaper. Sharp dispatchers will always scan the real estate section and the public announcements of the local zoning board decisions to pick up on new developments. Particular attention, naturally, should be paid to changes in a potential life hazard (a big old New Englander, occupied for years by two sisters, is sold and converted into four apartments; or a hospital closes, leaving a large vacant building with nowhere near its previous life hazard) and changes in fire loading (the storage of volatile chemicals in occupancies not previously used for that purpose; or a former dry cleaners becomes an ice cream parlor).

Consider taking these bits of pertinent information and keying them to either alarm assignment cards or computer-generated prompts. Dispatchers and responding companies must be aware of them. If you keep current on what's happening in your jurisdiction, you may discover a need for additions or improvements in the other area of operations planning:

2) Available resources to meet emergencies—You must regularly ask yourself, your dispatchers, your firefighters, your superiors, and your colleagues from other jurisdictions, Is what we have to work with sufficient to meet the demands that are going to be placed on us?

In this regard, you have to be especially wary of ignorance. What you don't know *can* hurt you! There is no way of knowing whether operations can be improved if you don't keep in touch with new developments in the field. This means attending conferences, paying visits to other jurisdictions, and—most importantly—keeping up with the literature in the field.

• Attending Conferences: These are not just opportunities to drink beer and swap stories. Vendors attend conferences. Seize the opportunity to receive hands-on experience with new equipment. Ask the sales reps your toughest questions, especially,

Can you give me the names of *all* the departments that are using your product? ("all" meaning not just the ones who are happy with the product). If you are seriously considering purchase, you'll want to contact the buyers yourself for their opinions, circumstances, and suggestions and then make your own determination. You'll want to ask the buyers if they're satisfied with the item, how they came to their purchase decision, and what changing conditions in their jurisdiction caused them to begin looking for something new. Were they made aware of an operational shortcoming by painful experience or did they simply have the foresight to assess their response capability in a changing protection area? Conferences are also useful places to make personal contacts with folks who come from a little farther away than your mutual-aid areas. They may have a better way of doing things of which you are not yet aware. They may be able to tell you what products and services to avoid in your operations planning.

• Visiting other operations: Your visits will have a lot of the same benefits derived from meeting conference attendees, but you'll get to see them and their equipment in action. You may especially want to visit areas that have undergone growth and change patterns similar to yours and see how they have handled it. New highway in the area? Are your power spreaders and cutters positioned for a speedy response to that area? Does your department need an additional power rescue tool to cope with the additional traffic because sending the unit that carries your only tool will strip a residential neighborhood of its truck company? Is there a new high-rise residence in your jurisdiction? Are your dispatchers aware of the floor plans and the apartment-numbering patterns? Has your airport expanded? Is there a need for a "hot line" to the tower or to the foam storage depots? Is there a new med-evac helicopter at the local hospital? Are you capable of speaking on the same frequency? Visiting folks who have had to cope with such issues will help. Remember, you gain just as much good in learning how *not* to do something.

• Keeping up with professional literature: The professional journals are most likely to have the newest information for your planning decisions. For the amount of useful data most of them provide, their cost is extremely low. They provide a forum for ideas, a place to ask for help as well as to receive it, and, unlike structured conferences, are available to you at your convenience.

Of course, as you move through operations planning, you will also be regularly uncovering new needs for the next planning concern:

Training. This area naturally covers all the other areas. If there are to be changes in your physical plant, there may well be changes in the training needs of the people who work there. These may include change in maintenance or oversight routines, different protocols for plant security, or any other issue related to the new aspects of the building.

If there are new personnel procedures, be they changes in the format for requesting time off, calling in sick, qualifying for promotion, or reporting injuries, both your dispatchers and their supervisors are going to need familiarization with these alterations. If your quality assurance studies repeatedly show substandard performance by dispatchers on such routine procedures as notifications or record keeping, some of your training plans will likely be devoted to techniques of supervision.

Your training regimen in the area of operations offers the opportunity for some of the most varied and interesting sessions for your dispatchers. It should include field experience if possible. The more your dispatchers know about both their protection area and the equipment they'll be sending to emergencies in that area, the better. Another interesting exercise is the area quiz. Give your dispatchers a map of an intersection or area and see if they can pencil in their dispatching concerns about that area. These may include occupancies, special life hazards, pipelines, power lines, highway intersection ramps, or subway routes. You can also ask specific questions on each map quiz: At what time of day does this area present the most life hazards? What's the greatest likelihood of fire/least likelihood of false alarm? In rural areas without hydrant systems, what's the nearest water source? Who are the first-due companies? Where's the nearest tower ladder? What police agency covers this area?

When planning the training for new equipment, find out if the vendor will provide it as part of the purchase deal. If you find that your dispatchers are going to need new fluencies—foreign language, haz-mat, or nuclear—take the steps necessary to ensure that they acquire them. I know of at least one area where representatives of the local power company assisted in training the area's dispatchers in the terminology they needed to know to understand the situations described to them by the nearby nuclear plant operators. This same type of shared familiarity can be accomplished with assistance from representatives of utilities, departments, and companies whose facilities present potential operating concerns for your department. It is helpful if your dispatchers are speaking the same language as callers who are talking about above-ground wires, power substations, pole-mounted transformers, manholes, sewer tunnels, bulk oil storage plants, railyards, airports, municipal incinerators, solid waste transfer stations, or any potential life hazard or source of heavy fire loading.

Schools and hospitals are sometimes comprised of many different structures spread out in a campus-type setting. Knowing the names of the buildings and what takes place in them is most useful for emergency communications personnel. The early Sunday morning call claiming that "there's smoke coming out of the Hoagland Building at Long Island College Hospital" might cause a great deal of concern among dispatchers unfamiliar with the area. That concern and the subsequent dispatching decision-making processes would be considerably different if it were known that the Hoagland Building houses a medical library and thus presents far less life hazard than a patient area of the hospital. Additionally, the likelihood of many people in the building early on a Sunday morning would be slim. Finally, if your plans included training sessions dedicated to the protocols surrounding these occupancies, your dispatchers would know who to contact at the hospital to get some idea of the number of employees who would be in the building at that time.

When planning with a large employer, you may find that they have the capacity to generate a lot of useful data—only sometimes they don't realize its usefulness to you. I'm familiar with a hospital that has a computerized timecard system capable of printing out the names of all on-duty employees at a given time. While the employer uses this data for its own specific purposes, it is as useful to a fire department as a riding list is to a company officer. You can take attendance and get an immediate idea of life hazard.

Anytime there is an addition to your Operations Manual, training should accompany the change. Therefore, if you are contemplating amendments to your manuals, you should also be planning for the training that goes with them. Of course, unless you significantly alter the budget process in your department, there's not a lot of training in that area. There is, however, one important integration of budget and the training function—the development of basic financial management skills for recently promoted personnel. Especially when dealing with a first step in a career ladder, where the promotee comes from an entry-level rank in which budget was not a concern, there will be a need for education in this area.

Planning is an all-encompassing activity at the heart of the fire service. It is both an operational and a management activity. That should have been obvious as you read through this book: Planning is intertwined throughout every chapter. Just to keep your perspective fresh, I suggest that you return to previous sections of this book as you do your planning. Think of this book as the skeleton upon which to build. The planning you do—how you apply what you learn and what you think of—is the muscle that makes the skeleton work. Once you've got that muscle, keep at it. Don't let your operation get flabby. If you are diligent, the people you protect will have available to them the kind of organization and operational strength they need to keep safe.

INDEX